ESSENTIAL ELEMENTS FOR CHOIR - BOOK ONE

ESSENTIAL MUSICIANSHIP

A COMPREHENSIVE CHORAL METHOD

VOICE • THEORY • SIGHT-READING • PERFORMANCE

BY
EMILY CROCKER
AND
JOHN LEAVITT

Essential Musicianship Consultants and Authors of *Essential Repertoire*
Glenda Casey
Bobbie Douglass
Jan Juneau
Janice Killian
Michael O'Hern
Linda Rann
Brad White

To the Student

Welcome to Essential Musicianship! We are pleased that you have chosen to participate in choral singing. With practice and dedication, you'll enjoy a lifetime of musical performance. Best wishes for your musical success!

ISBN 978-0-7935-4329-8

HAL•LEONARD®
CORPORATION
7777 W. BLUEMOUND RD. P.O. BOX 13819 MILWAUKEE, WI 53213

TABLE OF CONTENTS AND OVERVIEW OF THE PROGRAM

Introduction vi

EE1 1
Voice: Posture • Breath • Tone..1
Theory: Rhythm • Beat • Note values (quarter, half, whole) 2
Sight-Reading: Rhythm drills (quarter, half, whole notes) 4

EE2 5
Voice: Five basic vowels (ee, eh, ah, oh, oo) 5
Theory: Basic notation (staff, clefs, note names) 7
Sight-Reading: Pitch drills 9

EE3 10
Voice: Breath support (diaphragm) 10
Theory: Measure • meter • barlines 12
Sight-Reading: Rhythm practice • Pitch practice 13
Performance: Speech Chorus:
    The Months of the Year 15

EE4 16
Voice: Review 16
Theory: Review 17
Sight-Reading: Rhythm practice • Pitch practice 18
Performance: Speech Chorus
    Tongue Twister 21

EE5 22
Voice: Practice (posture, breath and vowel shape) 22
Theory: Pitch • Scale • Key of C major 24
Sight-Reading: Pitch drills • Combine rhythm and pitch 25
Performance: Short songs with text • accompanied song
    Proverbs (unison) 28
    Follow Me (unison) 29

EE6 31
Voice: Practice (posture, breath, and vowel shape) 31
Theory: Whole steps and half steps..33
Sight-Reading: Whole/half step drill and exercises.............................34
Performance: Singing in parts...36
    Treble 37
    Tenor Bass 38
    Mixed...39

TABLE OF CONTENTS AND OVERVIEW OF THE PROGRAM

EE7 41
Voice: Practice (posture, breath, and vowel shape) 41
Theory: Review 43
Sight-Reading: Practice (pitch and rhythm) 44
Performance: a cappella songs (C major) 47
    Treble: Sing Alleluia 48
    Tenor Bass: Sing Alleluia 49
    Mixed: Winter 50

EE8 52
Voice: Practice (posture, breath, vowels) • articulation 52
Theory: Sharps and flats • Key of G major...54
Sight-Reading: Pitch drill • Exercises 56
Performance: a cappella songs...58
    Treble: Erin 59
    Tenor Bass: Shipwrecked 60
    Mixed: Sing Your Songs..61

EE9 62
Voice: Practice (posture, breath, vowels, articulation)............................62
Theory: Accidentals • Key signature...64
Sight-Reading: Pitch drills • Exercises 66
Performance: a cappella canon 67
    Joyfully Sing (3-Part, any combination) 68

EE10 69
Voice: The Breathing Process 69
Theory: Rests (quarter, half, whole)...71
Sight-Reading: Rhythm drills with rests 72
Performance: Speech chorus
    Animal Song (4-Part, any combination) 73

EE11 74
Voice: Review...74
Theory: Review 75
Sight-Reading: Exercises 76
Performance: accompanied song
    Rain (unison) 77

TABLE OF CONTENTS AND OVERVIEW OF THE PROGRAM

EE12 79
Voice: Vocalization 79
Theory: Melodic intervals 81
Sight-Reading: Melodic interval practice (C major, G major) 82
Performance: a cappella songs
   Treble: Sing Hosanna 85
   Tenor Bass: Sing Hosanna 85
   Mixed: Sing Hosanna 86

EE13 87
Voice: Review of vowels • Additional vowel sounds 87
Theory: Harmonic intervals 89
Sight-Reading: Practice with harmonic intervals 90
Performance: accompanied song
   Dance! (SA, TB or SATB) 92

EE14 95
Voice: The neutral vowel (ə) 95
Theory: Triads • The Tonic Chord 97
Sight-Reading: Tonic chord practice 99
Performance: a cappella songs
   Treble: Spring Quiet..101
   Tenor Bass: Sons of Art 103
   Mixed: O Music, Sweet Music..105

EE15 107
Voice: Review 107
Theory: Review • "Pickup" notes 108
Sight-Reading: Tonic chord practice 109
Performance: accompanied songs 110
   Treble: King William...111
   Tenor Bass: King William 113
   Mixed: Hosanna 115

EE16 118
Voice: Diphthongs 118
Theory: Key of F major • Dotted half notes 121
Sight-Reading: Chord drills • Exercises in $\frac{3}{4}$ and $\frac{4}{4}$ 122
Performance: a cappella songs...124
   Treble: Love In Thy Youth 125
   Tenor Bass: As The Holly Groweth Green 127
   Mixed: The Call 129

CONTENTS

TABLE OF CONTENTS AND OVERVIEW OF THE PROGRAM

EE17 130
Voice: Articulation ("t" and "d") 130
Theory: Eighth notes and rests • Beat/division of beat 132
Sight-Reading: Rhythm drills...134
Performance: speech chorus
   Hey Diddle Diddle! (2-Part, any combination)..135

EE18 137
Voice: Review..137
Theory: Review 138
Sight-Reading: Practice...139
Performance: a cappella songs
   Treble: Let Us Chase The Squirrel...140
   Tenor Bass: Leave Her, Johnny...142
   Mixed: Betty Botter 144

EE19 145
Voice: Articulation (singing "r")...145
Theory: Meter • Downbeat/Secondary stress 147
Sight-Reading: Practice with changing meters 148
Performance: a cappella song
   Alleluia (SA, TB or SATB) 149

EE20 152
Voice: Comprehensive Review...152
Theory: Comprehensive Review 153
Performance: accompanied songs
   Treble: O Soldier, Soldier 155
   Tenor Bass: The Hunt...159
   Mixed: The Bells 162

Appendix..166
Rhythm Drills...173
Pitch Drills 176
About The Authors 178

TO THE TEACHER

ESSENTIAL MUSICIANSHIP – BOOK ONE and the subsequent Volumes 2 and 3 are designed to provide a basis for developing comprehensive musicianship within the choral rehearsal through a sequenced study of *voice, music theory,* and the practical application of both in *music reading* skills.

For students to gain the most from this course of study, plan 10-15 minutes of daily study, including practice/review and introducing new material.

Features of the Program
• The sequence is pedagogically sound and practical. The necessary elements for good choral singing are systematically presented.

• The terminology is accurate and literal.

• Vocal pedagogy and music theory are presented in a format that is ideal for introducing important musical concepts within the choral rehearsal.

• The method is designed to help students become independent thinkers and to constantly apply their learning to an ever-widening set of musical experiences.

• It provides a ready-made resource of choral concepts and repertoire presented in a practical sequence that is ideal for both beginning and experienced teachers.

• It is designed to be successful within a variety of choral organizations: treble, tenor-bass, mixed.

• The concepts presented are structured so as to allow students to discover their individual potential. The material is score-oriented, i.e., the students are led to discover the meaning of music both through experiencing it and interpreting it through the medium of the printed page. This process of converting "symbol to sound" and "sound to symbol" is at the heart of becoming a musically literate individual.

Combining ESSENTIAL MUSICIANSHIP with ESSENTIAL REPERTOIRE
This book may be presented in conjunction with any of the four levels of *ESSENTIAL REPERTOIRE,* twelve volumes of high quality, time-tested choral literature for mixed, treble and tenor bass choirs.

For each choral selection in *ESSENTIAL REPERTOIRE,* the authors have provided complete lesson plans including:
• Objectives
• Historical/stylistic guidelines and cultural context
• Choral techniques (warm-ups, exercises, drills)
• Rehearsal and performance tips
• Assessment techniques and enrichment ideas

Together with *ESSENTIAL MUSICIANSHIP,* these books provide a complete curriculum for the choral experience.

HOW TO USE THIS BOOK

Book 1 is organized into twenty segments (chapters), each including material for developing skills in voice, theory, sight-reading, and performance.

The material in each segment has been systematically developed to integrate all the skills of a choral musician. How long to remain within a single segment will depend on a variety of circumstances, including the age and experience level of the students and how often the group meets.

Allow approximately 15 minutes of a 1-hour rehearsal to be devoted to the "voice/theory/sight-reading" portions of this material. This need not be approached as a block section of the rehearsal, but can be integrated throughout the lesson in shorter sessions to heighten students' interest.

Each day's material should be balanced between review/practice and presenting new material. Before proceeding to the next chapter, evaluate the students' comprehension and mastery of the material.

Voice

Each segment provides material to help a young singer learn and apply the techniques of good singing, and particularly emphasizes the importance of:
- Good posture
- Expanded rib cage breathing, breath support, learning to sustain a phrase
- Tone production, choral blend, vertical vowel formation, diphthongs, word stress
- Diction, articulation of consonants

Theory

Each segment presents music theory concepts in a clear and concise manner. Appropriate drill is included and "check your knowledge" questions are presented in each chapter for a quick evaluation of knowledge-based material. Specific concepts are highlighted at the top of each page and in the table of contents/sequence overview on p. ii.

Sight-Reading

The sight-reading drills and exercises are designed to allow the students to practice the concepts presented in the theory section of the chapter. Keep in mind that as the students practice particular drills they are internalizing that aural skill and synthesizing it with other musical concepts they have experienced.

The sight-reading drills include:
- Basic familiarity with musical terms and symbols
- Note identification
- Drills for echo-singing and group practice
- Combinable exercises that provide practice in unison sight-reading and part-singing

HOW TO USE THIS BOOK

(continued)

When working on the sight-reading material, always be musical when demonstrating and performing a particular phrase or pattern. Apply sight-reading skills in every area of music-making.

Performance

Each chapter includes repertoire that applies and reinforces the concepts presented in each chapter. These songs, written for treble, tenor-bass, and mixed ensembles provide:
- Resources for developing reading skills, and the application of musical concepts
- Resources for developing musicianship and expressive singing
- Concert level repertoire that includes quality texts, a balance of styles, harmonic, melodic and rhythmic aspects of music-making (canons, counterpoint, expressive and satisfying melodies, speech choruses), and interesting musical forms
- A balance of repetition/patterning and experience with more challenging material

Music History

Throughout the text, short informational sections are included to help put the material presented into a historical context. This supplementary material helps students to see their own role as choral musicians now and as a part of a rich and rewarding tradition.

Methods of Sight-Reading

There are many good methods to use in developing sight-reading skills. They all have advantages and drawbacks. In selecting a method to follow, consider the following:
- Age and experience of the singers
- Methods used by other musical organizations in your school or district
- Methods familiar to your students
- Your own background and training

Remember, it is not *which* method you choose, but rather that it is employed consistently and daily. An overview of several common sight-reading methods for both pitch and rhythm are described in the appendix, beginning on page 167.

A teacher's edition is available for each of the three volumes of *ESSENTIAL MUSICIANSHIP*. It includes a more complete overview of the course, and detailed lesson plans for presenting the material. See page 178 for a full series listing.

POSTURE/BREATH/TONE

Posture: A good singing posture helps produce good breathing for singing. An effective singing posture includes the following:

- Stand with feet apart
- Knees unlocked
- Back straight
- Head erect
- Rib cage lifted
- Shoulders relaxed
- Hands at your side

Standing posture   Raising the rib cage

1. To help develop good posture for singing, practice this exercise: Place your fingertips on the crown of your head (elbows out). Notice how your rib cage is raised. Slowly open your arms and continue in a downward arc until they rest at your sides. Try to maintain the raised rib cage as you lower your arms.

Breath: An expanded rib cage increases breath capacity and provides the basis for a free, relaxed and pleasing vocal tone. The following exercise will help you expand the rib cage and take a full breath for singing.

2. Raise your arms overhead slowly while inhaling, then exhale your air on a "ss" while slowly lowering your arms to their original position. Try to maintain the raised rib cage while lowering your arms.

Tone: While you use your voice everyday for communication, singing requires a different way of producing a sound. A "yawn-sigh" is a very useful exercise that helps prepare the voice to produce a full, relaxed, free and pleasing tone.

3. Yawn-sigh — Yawn, then starting on a high pitch, produce a relaxed descending vocal sigh on an "ah" vowel, somewhat like a siren.

RHYTHM

Rhythm is the organization of sound length (duration).

Beat is a steadily recurring pulse.

Rhythm Practice:
Practice keeping a steady beat as a group. Clap, tap, or chant with a clock or metronome.

Note values: Three common note values are the *quarter* note, the *half* note, and the *whole* note.

Quarter note   Half note   Whole note

In most of the music that we'll begin with, the quarter note will be assigned the beat.

You'll notice from the chart below that *two quarter notes* have the same duration as *one half note*, and that *two half notes* (or four quarters) have the same duration as *one whole note*.

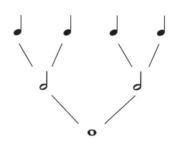

Check Your Knowledge!
1. What is *rhythm*?

2. What is a *beat*?

3. Identify the following notes: ♩   𝅗𝅥   𝅝

4. How many quarter notes equal the same duration as a half note?

5. How many half notes equal the same duration as a whole note?

6. How many quarter notes equal the same duration as a whole note?

RHYTHM PRACTICE

Identify these note values. Practice aloud by echoing your teacher.

 RHYTHM PRACTICE

Read each line (clap, tap, or chant). Concentrate on keeping a steady beat. Repeat as necessary until you've mastered the exercise.

POSTURE/BREATH/TONE

Posture: Review the steps for a good singing posture. Remember that a good posture helps produce good breathing for singing.

- Stand with feet apart
- Knees unlocked
- Back straight
- Head erect
- Rib cage lifted
- Shoulders relaxed
- Hands at your side

Breath: Remember that an expanded rib cage helps develop expanded breath capacity. Practice the following exercises:

1. Raise your arms overhead slowly while inhaling, then exhale your air on a "ss" while slowly lowering your arms to their original position. Try to maintain the raised rib cage while lowering your arms.

2. Repeat Exercises #1, but exhale with 4 short "ss" sounds followed by a longer "ss" sound:

   ss ss ss ss ss_____ (repeat once or twice in one breath)

3. Imagine there is a milkshake as large as the room. Hold your arms out from your body as if you were holding the giant milkshake and "drink" the air through a giant straw. Exhale on a yawn-sigh.

Tone: *Vowels* are the basis for a good choral tone, so make sure that you sing all vowels with a *relaxed jaw*, a *vertical mouth shape*, and with *space inside your mouth*. This helps each singer to produce a full and free vocal tone quality that blends well with other voices to create a pleasing choral sound.

The *five basic vowels* include:

ee   eh   ah   oh   oo

Notice that each vowel sound is produced with a relaxed and vertical dropped jaw.

 POSTURE/BREATH/TONE

At this time, we'll focus on the "ah" vowel. Here are several exercises to apply the principle of the *relaxed jaw* and *vertical mouth shape*:

4. Sing the following exercise with a relaxed jaw. Hold the last note and listen to see that you are producing a full, blended choral sound that is in tune with the voices around you. Repeat at different pitch levels both higher and lower, and use the different text syllables as indicated.

nah   nah   nah   nah   nah   nah   nah
mah   mah   mah   mah   mah   mah   mah
yah   yah   yah   yah   yah   yah   yah

5. Sing the following exercise first with 1 text syllable for each separate note and then 1 text syllable for two notes slurred (connected) together. Repeat at different pitch levels both higher and lower.

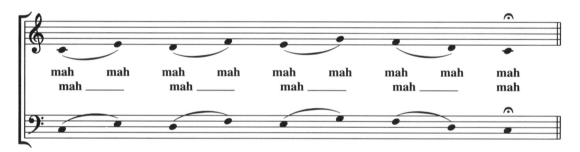

mah   mah   mah   mah   mah   mah   mah   mah   mah
mah _____   mah _____   mah _____   mah _____   mah

6. Sing "America." Notice how many "ah" vowels appear in the text. NOTE: Some of these vowels are part of a vowel blend (also called a *diphthong*). For example, "my" is really two vowel sounds: ah + ee. Concentrate primarily on the "ah" of this diphthong.
   • Maintain a dropped jaw for all vowels and especially the "ah."
   • Take a full expanded rib cage breath. Can you sing a whole phrase in one breath?

    (ah)(ah)   (ah)   (ah)   (ah)   (ah)
(breathe) My country 'tis of thee, sweet land of liberty, of thee I sing.

        (ah)(ah)   (ah)   (ah)   (ah)
(breathe) Land where my fathers died, Land of the pilgrims' pride,

     (ah)   (ah)   (ah)   (ah)
(breathe) From ev'ry mountainside, let freedom ring.

BASIC NOTATION

A *staff* is a graph of 5 lines and 4 spaces on which music is written. The staff shown below is a *grand staff*. A grand staff is a grouping of two staves.

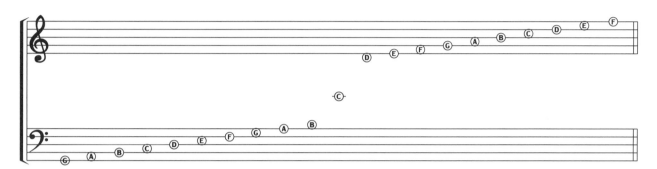

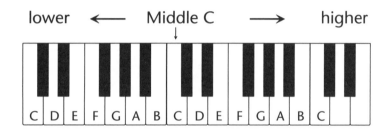

Notice the two symbols at the beginning of the staves on the left hand side. These are called clefs. A *clef* is a symbol that identifies a set of pitches. The *Treble Clef* generally refers to pitches higher than middle C. The *Bass Clef* generally refers to pitches lower than middle C. Notice that middle C has its own little line and may be written in either clef – either at the bottom of the treble clef or the top of the bass clef.

Treble Clef (G Clef)
Second line is G
(The curve of the Clef
loops around the G line.)

Bass Clef (F Clef)
Fourth line is F
(The dots of the clef surround
the F line.)

An easy way to learn the notes on the treble clef staff is to remember that the spaces spell the word *FACE* from the bottom up. An easy way to learn the notes on the bass clef staff is to remember that the spaces spell *ACEG* or *All Cows Eat Grass*. Make up your own phrase for the acronym *GBDFA* (for the bass clef lines) and *EGBDF* (for the treble clef lines).

Check your knowledge!

1. What is the name of the graph of lines and spaces on which music is written?

2. How many lines and spaces does this graph have?

3. What is the name of the symbol used to describe a set of pitches? Name two types of these symbols.

4. Give another name for *G Clef*. Give another name for *F Clef*.

5. Name the pitch which may be written on its own little line in either clef.

Practice
Name the notes in the following examples.

 PRACTICE—NOTE IDENTIFICATION

Practice echo-singing these notes by letter name.

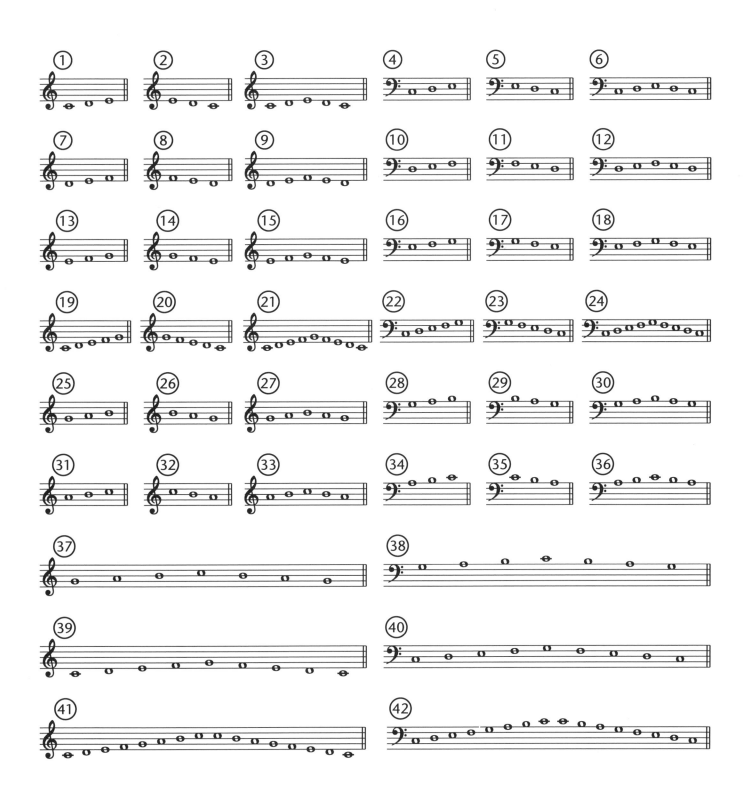

POSTURE/BREATH

Posture: Review the steps to a good singing posture.

- Stand with feet apart
- Knees unlocked
- Back straight
- Head erect
- Rib cage lifted
- Shoulders relaxed
- Hands at your side

Breath: Remember that a lifted and expanded rib cage helps to develop expanded breath capacity. When you sing a musical phrase supported by a good singing breath, you are demonstrating good breath support.

1. Bend at the waist and pick an imaginary flower. Inhale the "fragrance" while slowly standing up. Exhale on a yawn-sigh.

Diaphragmatic Breathing: One aspect of breath support is the lifted and expanded rib cage. Another aspect of breath support is the process of activating the *diaphragm*. The diaphragm is a muscle just below the lungs that moves downward during inhalation as the rib cage expands and air fills the lungs. Exercises which help you become aware of this action of the diaphragm can help you learn to energize and enrich the vocal sound you are producing.

2. When people are surprised or frightened, they usually take in a rapid breath with a noticeable movement of the diaphragm. Place your hand just below your rib cage and above your waist and then take a "surprised breath."
   • Do you feel the movement?
   • Did your hand move as a result of the surprised breath?

3. See if you can produce the same movement of the diaphragm as in #2 in the following exercise. Use short *whispered* sounds, no voice.

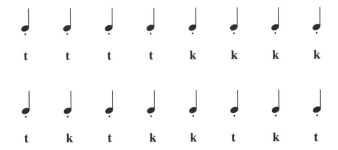

BREATH/TONE

4. Practice the following exercise, keeping the sounds short and detached. Use the diaphragm as in #3 to support and energize the tone. Repeat at different pitch levels, both higher and lower:

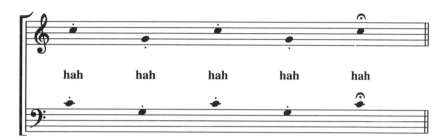

hah hah hah hah hah

5. Do the exercise above, but this time use an "oo" vowel. Remember to keep a relaxed jaw, vertical mouth position, and space inside the mouth.
   • Keep the sounds short and detached.
   • Support the tone by activating the diaphragm.

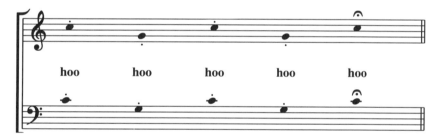

hoo hoo hoo hoo hoo

6. In the following exercise, sing the musical pitches so they are smooth and connected.
   • Take a full expanded rib cage breath supported by the action of the diaphragm (even though in this exercise the notes are connected and not short).
   • Sing the "oo" vowel with rounded lips, a relaxed jaw, and vertical space inside the mouth.
   • Repeat at different pitch levels, both higher and lower.

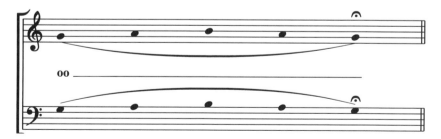

oo

MEASURES • METERS • BARLINES

Barlines are vertical lines that divide the staff into smaller sections called measures. A *double barline* indicates the end of a section or piece of music.

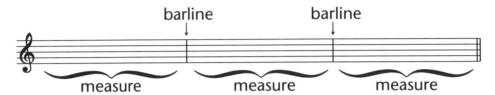

Meter is a form of rhythmic organization. For example:

4 = Four beats per measure (♩ ♩ ♩ ♩)
4 = The quarter note (♩) receives the beat.

3 = Three beats per measure (♩ ♩ ♩)
4 = The quarter note (♩) receives the beat.

2 = Two beats per measure (♩ ♩)
4 = The quarter note (♩) receives the beat.

The numbers that identify the meter are called the *time signature*. The time signature is placed after the clef at the beginning of a song or section of a song.

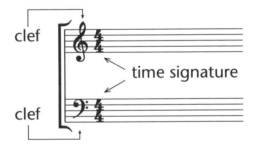

Check your knowledge!
1. What are the vertical lines that divide a staff into smaller sections called?

2. Name the smaller divided sections of a staff.

3. What is a *double barline*?

4. Describe *meter*.

5. What are the numbers that identify the meter called?

6. Describe the following meters: $\frac{4}{4}$ $\frac{3}{4}$ $\frac{2}{4}$

RHYTHM PRACTICE

Clap, tap, or chant.

①

②

③

④

⑤

⑥

⑦

⑧

⑨

PITCH REVIEW

Echo sing or sing as a group.

MUSICAL TERMS

History: The piano, a stringed instrument whose strings are struck by hammers activated by keys, was developed in the 18th century and originally called the pianoforte, an Italian term meaning "soft-loud." It was called this because unlike an earlier keyboard instrument called the harpsichord, the loudness of the piano's sound could be varied by the touch of the fingers.

Musical Terms

p - piano; soft

f - forte; loud

Apply what you've learned about music reading to this short speech chorus.
- After you sight-read the rhythm, repeat with the printed text.
- Repeat as necessary for accuracy.

The Months Of The Year

REVIEW/PRACTICE

In group discussion, answer the following questions, giving examples or illustrating where possible. Refer to VOICE-BUILDERS in Chapters 1-3 as needed.

1.   Describe the steps to a good singing posture.

2.   How does good posture affect singing?

3.   How does an expanded rib cage affect breathing?

4.   What is a yawn-sigh?

5.   List the five basic vowels.

6.   Describe three things you should do to produce the basic mouth position in singing the five basic vowels.

7.   What is the basic vowel sound in the word "from." Describe or illustrate the basic mouth position for singing this vowel.

8.   Describe two aspects of breath support.

9.   What is the muscle called that is below the lungs and that moves downward during inhalation?

10. What is the basic vowel sound in the word "who." Describe or illustrate the basic mouth position for singing this vowel.

History: The development of a simple and melodious vocal style of singing during the 17th century was called *bel canto,* from the Italian meaning "beautiful singing." Later, bel canto became associated not only with beauty of sound, but also with brilliant performance, especially in the operas of Mozart and Italian composers of the 18th century. One famous Mozart opera is *The Magic Flute.*

 REVIEW/PRACTICE

In group discussion, answer the following questions, giving examples or illustrating where possible. Refer to THEORY-BUILDERS in Chapters 1-3 as needed.

1. What is *rhythm*?

2. What is a steadily recurring pulse called?

3. Identify the following notes.

4. How many quarter notes equal a whole note? How many half notes equal a whole note?

5. How many lines are in a staff? How many spaces are in a staff?

6. What is a *clef*? Name two types of clefs.

7. Which clef is middle C written in?

8. What are *barlines*? What is a *double barline*?

9. Name a form of rhythmic organization.

10. What is a *time signature*? Name and describe three time signatures.

Matching

① 𝄢   a) quarter notes

② 𝄞   b) middle C

③ ♩ ♩ ♩ ♩   c) bass clef

④ 𝅝   d) treble clef

⑤ 𝅗𝅥 𝅗𝅥   e) half notes

⑥   f) time signature

⑦ 𝄴   g) whole note

RHYTHM PRACTICE

Clap, tap, or chant.

PITCH PRACTICE

Speak the following pitches, echo sing or sing as a group.

MORE PITCH PRACTICE

Name the following pitches, echo sing or sing as a group.

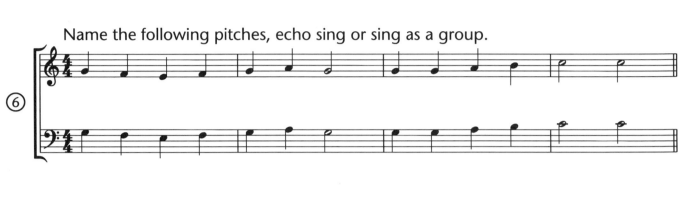

⑥

⑦

Name these pitches as above. Notice the more extreme range.

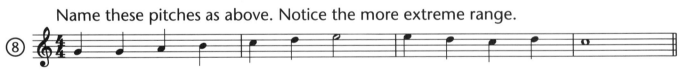

⑧

⑨

MUSICAL TERMS

Musical terms

cresc. — crescendo; an Italian word which means gradually louder.

Apply what you've learned about music reading to this short speech chorus.
• Sight-read the rhythm, and repeat as needed to become accurate.
• Repeat with the printed text.

Tongue Twister

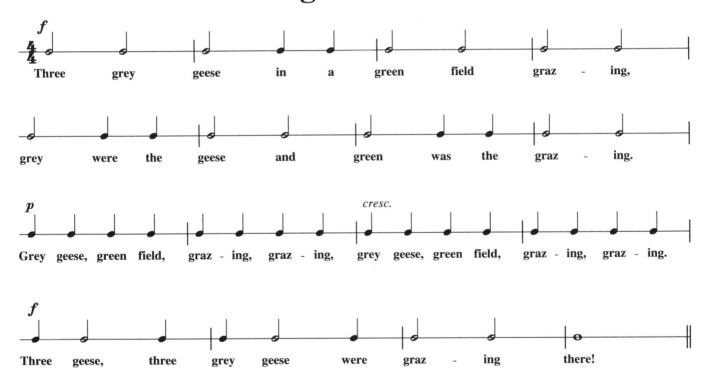

POSTURE/BREATH/TONE

Posture: Review the steps to a good singing posture.
- Stand with feet apart
- Knees unlocked
- Back straight
- Head erect
- Rib cage lifted
- Shoulders relaxed
- Hands at your side

Breath: Put your hands on the sides of your rib cage and inhale. Notice the movement of the rib cage. Breathe out on a whispered "ah."

Tone: The following exercises focus on the "oh" vowel. Notice in the illustration that the lips are more rounded than the "ah" vowel, but more open than the "oo" vowel. Remember to keep vertical space inside your mouth as you sing all these vowels:

ah

oh

oo

1. As you sing this exercise remember to:
   - Keep the sounds short and detached.
   - Support the tone by activating the diaphragm.
   - Repeat at different pitch levels, both higher and lower.

TONE

2. In the following exercise, sing the musical pitches so they are smooth and connected.
   • Take a full supported rib cage breath.
   • Sing the "oh" vowel with rounded lips and vertical space inside the mouth.
   • Sing the pitches so they are smooth and connected.

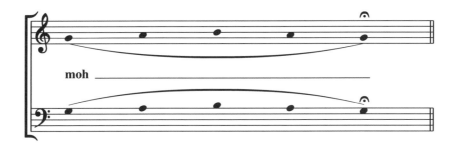

3. In the following exercise, connect two notes together on the syllable "moh." Be sure that your mouth doesn't change shape to an "oo" as you prepare to sing the consonant "m."

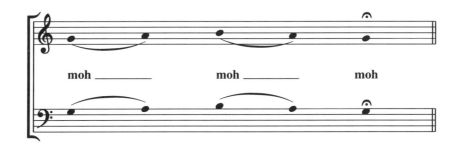

4. In the following exercise, each word uses an "oh" vowel.

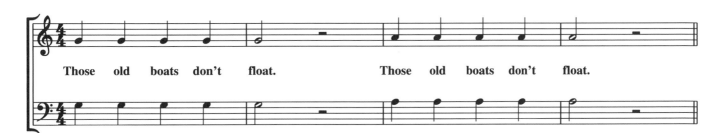

PITCH • SCALE • KEY OF C

Pitch — the highness or lowness of musical sound.

Scale — an inventory or collection of pitches. The word "scale" (from the Italian *scala*) means ladder. Thus, many musical scales are a succession of pitches higher and lower.

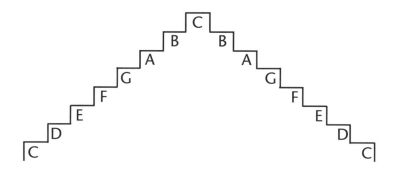

Key — The importance of one pitch over the others in a scale. Frequently, the key note or tone might be described as the home tone. In the Key of C, C is the home tone or keynote.

Key of C Scale

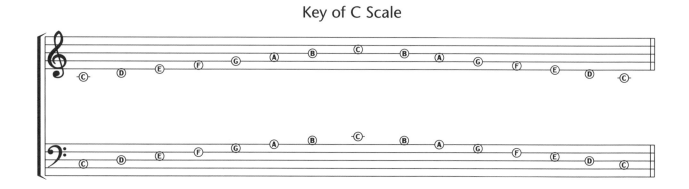

Check your knowledge!
1. What is *pitch*?

2. Define *scale*. Define *scala*.

3. Describe *key*. Describe *keynote*.

KEY OF C PRACTICE

Identify the following pitches in the key of C. Echo-sing these drills with your teacher.

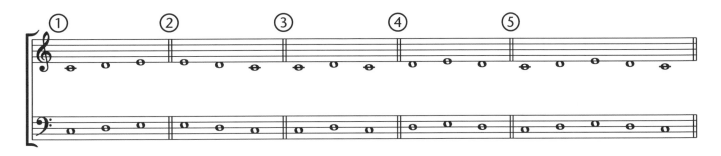

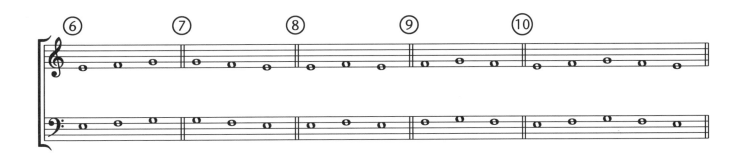

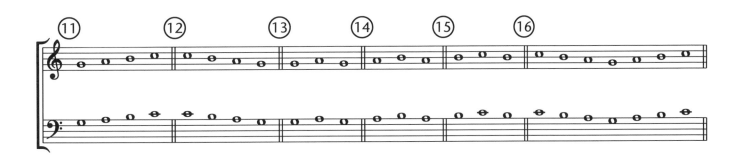

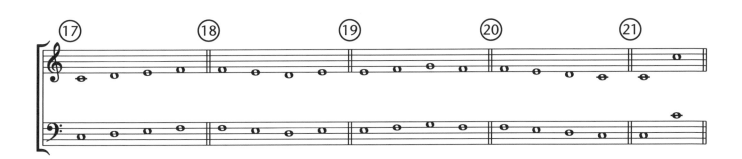

RHYTHM AND PITCH

History: Human voices are generally divided into four basic ranges:
soprano — the highest treble voice, usually written in treble clef
alto — a treble voice that is lower than the soprano, usually written in treble clef
tenor — a male voice written in bass clef or treble clef, that is higher than a bass voice
bass — a male voice written in bass clef that is lower than a tenor voice

The following exercises combine pitch and rhythm. Chant the rhythm first, then add the pitches. Repeat as necessary to master each drill.

(Remember to keep a steady beat)

MELODY • HARMONY

The following exercises combine pitch and rhythm. Chant the rhythm first, then add pitch. Repeat as necessary. When you've mastered all the exercises, you may sing the lines in any combination. For example, divide into two groups with one group singing #1 and the other group singing #2.

Each line sung by itself produces *melody* (a succession of musical tones). When two or more melodies are combined, the result is *harmony* (musical tones sounded simultaneously).

Apply what you've learned about music reading to these short songs.
- Chant the rhythm.
- Add pitch. Repeat as necessary for accuracy.
- Sing with text and expression.

Proverbs
For Unison voices a cappella

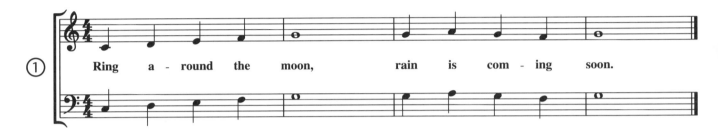

① Ring a - round the moon, rain is com - ing soon.

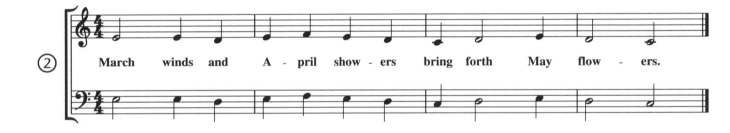

② March winds and A - pril show - ers bring forth May flow - ers.

③ Red sky at night, sail - ors' de - light,

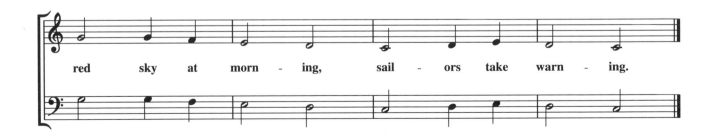

red sky at morn - ing, sail - ors take warn - ing.

UNISON VOICES

For extra challenge, here is a short song with piano accompaniment.
- Notice the piano part. The piece begins with 4 measures of piano accompaniment.
- Identify the vocal lines. In this piece, the vocal lines are indicated by arrows: →
- Sight-read the rhythm, then speak the pitch names.
- Sing the pitches and repeat as needed to become accurate.
- Add the printed text, then add the piano accompaniment. The voices enter on a C. Practice until you can enter on the correct note.
- Take full expanded rib cage breaths. Sing with expression!

Follow Me
For Unison voices and Piano

Words and Music by
EMILY CROCKER

POSTURE/BREATH/TONE

Posture: Check your posture and ask yourself these questions.
- Stand with feet apart (Is your weight balanced?)
- Knees unlocked (Can you bend them easily?)
- Back straight (Are you standing erect comfortably and not stiff?)
- Head erect (Is your chin level, and not too far up or down?)
- Rib cage lifted (Is your chest high and able to expand?)
- Shoulders relaxed (Are they comfortably down, not too far forward or back?)
- Hands at your side (Relaxed and free of tension)

Just like athletes, singers need to prepare themselves for the physical process of singing. Performance, whether on the playing field or in a concert, will suffer if the body is not sufficiently prepared or involved.

Practice good posture, good breathing, and good vocal habits every day in rehearsal, and these good habits will be there to help you succeed in performance.

1. Lift the left shoulder high and then let it fall. Repeat with the right shoulder and then both shoulders. Drop the head gently to the chest, and then let it roll to the right and then the left. Stretch overhead, then fall forward like a rag doll and then gradually stand up to a good singing posture.

Breath: Practice breathing exercises every day. Apply this practice to all your music making, sight-reading music, rehearsing music, performing music.

2. When people are suddenly startled, they usually take a deep natural breath very quickly. Take a "surprised" breath. Notice the action of the *diaphragm.*

3. Imagine that there is an elevator platform at the bottom of your lungs. Drop the platform toward the floor as you inhale. Inhale 4 counts, exhale 4 counts. Repeat with 5, then 6 counts.

Tone: Review the 5 basic vowels used in choral singing: ee, eh, ah, oh, oo. Most other vowel sounds are modifications or blends of these five sounds.

    ee   eh   ah   oh   oo

 TONE

4. Practice the following exercise and notice the difference between the vowels. With all the vowels remember to keep a relaxed jaw and vertical space inside the mouth.

   Especially on the "ee" and "eh" vowels, it is important to keep the corners of the mouth from spreading outward. If you sing the "ee" and "eh" vowel with a horizontal rather than a vertical mouth shape, it may sound flat and disrupt the tone quality you are trying to achieve.
   - For the "ee" vowel, keep the corners of your mouth tucked in.
   - For the "eh" vowel, the mouth is opened slightly more than the "ee".
   - For both, use space inside the mouth.
   - Repeat the exercise at different pitch levels, both higher and lower.

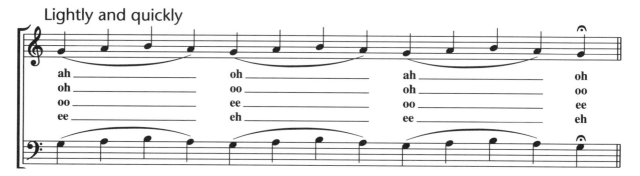

5. Practice the following descending scale.
   - Take an expanded rib cage breath and try to sing the entire pattern on one breath.
   - Keep a relaxed jaw and vertical space inside your mouth. Keep the corners of your mouth from spreading outward.
   - Change smoothly from one vowel to the next. Blend your voice with those around you.
   - Repeat at different pitch levels, both higher and lower.

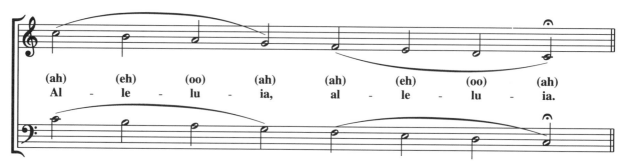

WHOLE STEPS • HALF STEPS

Remember that *key* is the importance of one pitch over the others in a scale. The keynote is described as the home tone. So far, we've learned the *key of C*, which if played on the piano would begin on C and progress stepwise using only the white keys of the piano.

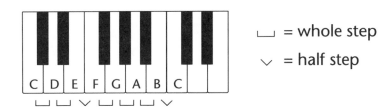

These steps on the piano for the key of C are an arrangement of *whole steps* and *half steps*.

A *half step* is the smallest distance (or *interval*) between two notes on a keyboard.

A *whole step* is the combination of two half steps side by side.

A *major scale* is a specific arrangement of whole steps and half steps in the following order:

C Major Scale

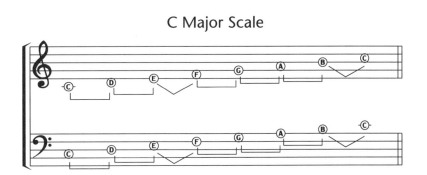

Check your knowledge!
1. What is a *half step*? What is a *whole step*?

2. What is a *major scale*?

3. What is the order of whole/half steps in a major scale?

WHOLE/HALF STEP PRACTICE

Sing notes and steps as indicated.

MORE WHOLE/HALF STEP PRACTICE

When the tenor part is written in treble clef, there is sometimes a small "8" attached to the clef sign (see #4 and #5 below). This means that the notes are to be sung 1 octave (8 scale tones) lower. Even when the "8" is missing from the clef sign, tenors sing an octave lower. For example:

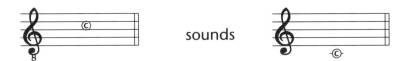

Sing each line separately and in any combination.

TREBLE • TENOR BASS • MIXED

The choral pieces on pages 37-40 were written for three different types of choral *ensembles*. An *ensemble* is a French term, and refers to a group of musicians performing together.
- Treble Chorus (soprano and alto)
- Tenor Bass Chorus (tenor and bass)
- Mixed Chorus (soprano, alto, tenor, bass)

Musical Terms:

slur - a curved line placed above or below a group of notes to indicate that they are to be sung on the same text syllable. Slurs are also used in instrumental music to indicate that the group of notes should be performed *legato* (or smooth and connected) or in the case of stringed instruments, with one stroke of the bow.

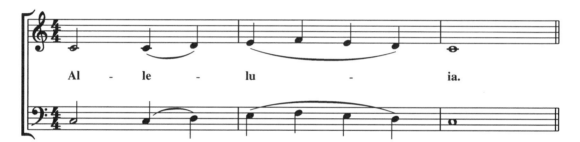

History: *Plainsong* or *Chant* was a style of singing which developed during the period of music history known as the Medieval era. A characteristic of Chant is the use of long groups of notes called *melismas* which were sung on one syllable, and often on the word "alleluia." These free-flowing melodies performed by solo voice (the *cantor*) and by the choir (the *schola*) were highly organized and structured, and important to the development of Western music. Chant continues to be a compositional device used by composers.

Chant exists in many non-Western cultures as well.

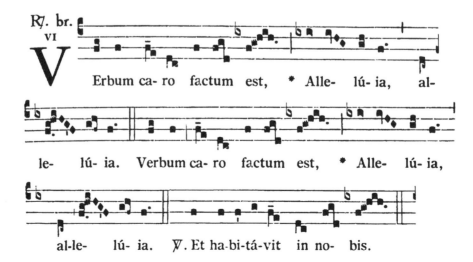

TREBLE CHORUS

First, sight-read the individual lines or *melodies*. Chant the rhythm first, then add pitch. Repeat as necessary. After you can sing each line separately, combine the lines. When two or more melodies are sung together, the result is *harmony*.

In the music below, lines #1 and #2 that you have just sung, are combined. Notice how the parts are bracketed together. Lines that are bracketed together are to be sung at the same time.

Now lines #1 and #2 are given text.

TENOR BASS CHORUS

First, sight-read the individual lines or *melodies*. Chant the rhythm first, then add pitch.
Repeat as necessary. After you can sing each line separately, combine the lines. When two or
more melodies are sung together, the result is *harmony*.

In the music below, lines #1 and #2 that you have just sung, are combined. Notice how the
parts are bracketed together. Lines that are bracketed together are to be sung at the same
time.

Now lines #1 and #2 are given text.

MIXED CHORUS

First, sight-read the individual lines or *melodies*. Chant the rhythm first, then add pitch. Repeat as necessary. After you can sing each line separately, combine the lines. When two or more melodies are sung together, the result is *harmony*.

In the music below, lines #1 through #4 that you have just sung, are combined. Notice how the parts are bracketed together. Lines that are bracketed together are to be sung at the same time.

NOTE: You may sing either SAT or SAB, if you lack sufficient voices for 4-part music.

MIXED CHORUS

Now lines #1 through #4 are given text.

NOTE: Throughout this text, for extra practice in sight-reading, treble choruses can sing the SA and Tenor Bass Choruses can sing the TB of the Mixed Chorus songs. Sopranos and Altos in Mixed Choirs can sight-read Treble Chorus songs, and Tenors and Basses can sight-read the TB material.

POSTURE/BREATH/TONE

Posture/ Breath:

1. Stretch overhead, side to side, up and down, then shake to relax any tight muscles.

2. Raise your arms overhead, stretching the fingers out in all directions. Bring the arms back to the side, relaxed and free of tension.

3. Exhale all your air. Wait for a moment until your body lets you know it needs air. Allow the air to flow in without effort. Repeat.

4. Imagine you have a milkshake as large as the room. Hold your arms in front of you around this giant "milkshake" and drink in the air through a giant "straw."

5. Place your fingertips just below your rib cage and take a "surprised" breath. Notice the movement of the diaphragm.

6. Inhale while raising your arms overhead (notice the expanded rib cage). Exhale on a hiss in this pattern, while slowly lowering your arms:

    ss   ss   ss   ss   ss _____ (repeat 1 or 2 times on each breath)

Tone: As you practice the following exercises, remember
- Keep a relaxed jaw and vertical space inside the mouth.
- Don't let the corners of the mouth spread outward.
- Listen, tune and blend your voice with other voices around you.
- Take a full, expanded rib cage breath before each repetition.
- Repeat at different pitch levels, both higher and lower.

7. Inhale while raising arms overhead and sing on "hoo" as you lower your arms. Sing short, detached sounds.

Lightly and detached

TONE

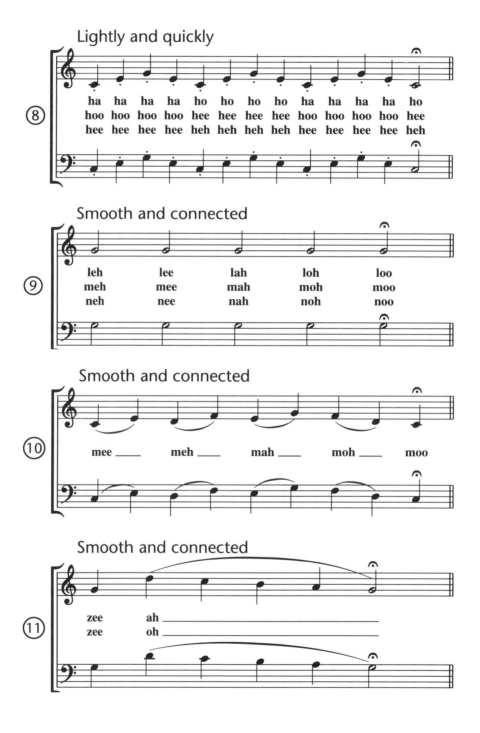

Check your knowledge!

1. What is *rhythm*?

2. Define *beat*.

3. How many half notes equal the same duration as a whole note?

4. How many quarter notes equal the same duration as a half note?

5. How many quarter notes equal the same duration as a whole note?

6. How many lines and spaces does a *staff* have?

7. Give another name for *G clef*. Give another name for *F clef*. Define both clefs.

8. Name the pitch which may be written on its own little line in either clef.

9. What are the vertical lines that divide a staff into smaller sections?

10. Name the smaller divided sections of a staff.

11. How can you tell the end of a section of a piece of music?

12. Describe *meter*. What are the numbers that identify the meter?

13. Describe the following meters: $\frac{4}{4}$ $\frac{3}{4}$ $\frac{2}{4}$

14. What is *pitch*?

15. Define *scale*. What is the Italian word for *scale* and its definition?

16. Describe *key*. Describe *keynote*.

17. What is *half step*? What is a *whole step*?

18. What is a major scale?

19. What is the order of whole/half steps in a major scale?

20. What is a *slur*?

21. What is an *octave*?

22. Define *soprano, alto, tenor, bass*.

REVIEW AND PRACTICE

Practice naming these notes.

Echo sing these pitches or sing as a group.

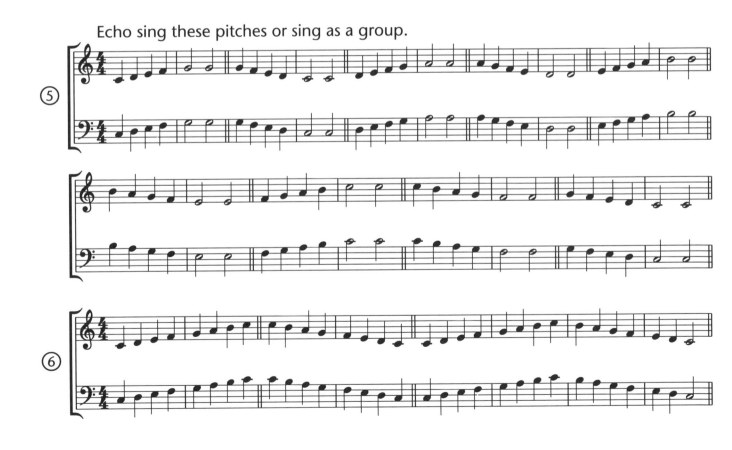

 REVIEW AND PRACTICE

Clap, tap, or chant (Can you describe these time signatures?)

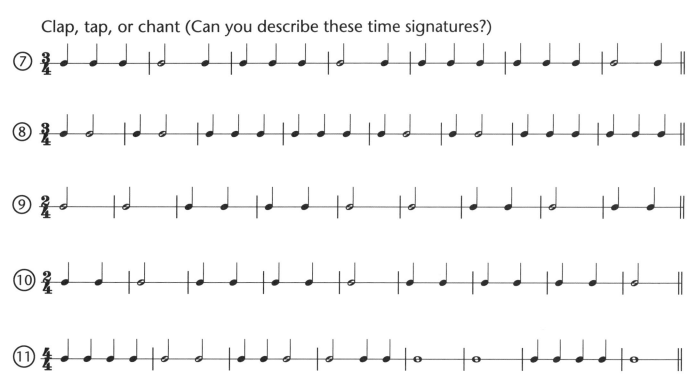

Whole/half step drill

REVIEW AND PRACTICE

Sing each line separately and in any combination.

MUSICAL TERMS

Musical Terms:

monophony – Music which consists of a single melody. From the Greek words meaning "one sound," *chant* or *plainsong* is monophony.

polyphony – Music that combines two or more simultaneous voice parts usually with different rhythms. From the Greek words meaning "many sounds," polyphony is sometimes called *counterpoint*.

homophony – Music which consists of two or more voice parts with similar or identical rhythms. From the Greek words meaning "same sounds," homophony could be described as being in "hymn-style."

Music History

Prior to 800 A.D. music was monophonic. The early stages of polyphony began in 800 A.D. and developed over the next several centuries. In the 18th century polyphony reached a high level of sophistication in the works of **Johann Sebastian Bach**.

Much music in the 19th Century (sometimes called the *Romantic Period*) was *homophonic*. Examples of homophonic music may be found in some of the piano works, songs, and choral works of **Frederick Chopin**, **Franz Schubert**, and **Johannes Brahms**.

TREBLE • TENOR BASS • MIXED

In the following short choral pieces for **Treble** and **Tenor Bass** Chorus, both entitled "Sing Alleluia," the style of the music is *polyphonic*; that is, the melodies of each part have different rhythms. In fact, the melodies even "cross" with the soprano going below the alto, and the tenor briefly going below the bass.

The piece for **Mixed** Chorus "Winter," is written in *homophonic* style; that is, the four parts have basically the same rhythm.

The author of the text of "Winter" is Alfred, Lord Tennyson (1850-1892), an English poet of the Romantic Period who often wrote on topics relating to nature.

As you sight-read these pieces, remember to:
• Chant the rhythm of each part. Repeat as needed to become accurate.
• Add the pitch. Repeat as needed.
• Combine the parts. Repeat as needed until secure.
• Add the printed text. Sing the dynamics and other musical style markings.
• Apply your knowledge of voice and use good breath support and tone quality. Listen for good intonation and blend.

TREBLE CHORUS

Remember to sing dynamics in your performance:

f – *forte*; loud

p – *piano*; soft

Sing Alleluia

For SA a cappella

Words and Music by
JOHN LEAVITT

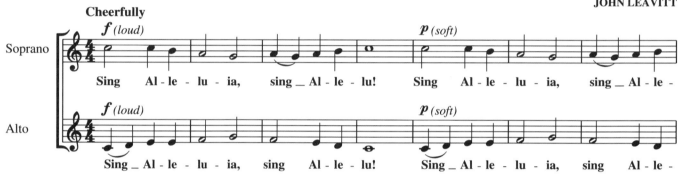

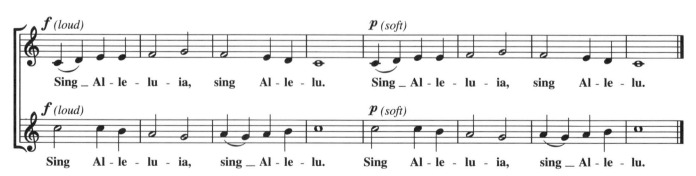

TENOR BASS CHORUS

Remember to sing dynamics in your performance:

f – *forte*; loud

p – *piano*; soft

Sing Alleluia

For TB a cappella

Words and Music by
JOHN LEAVITT

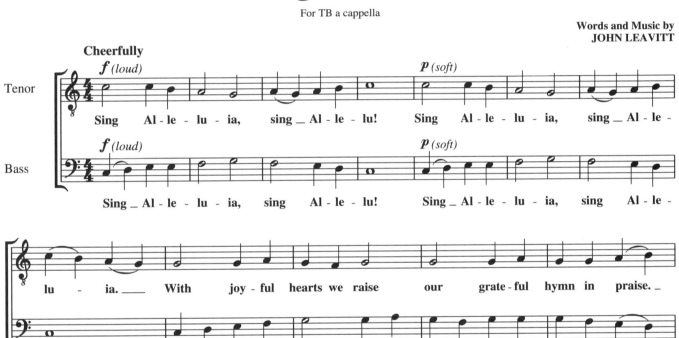

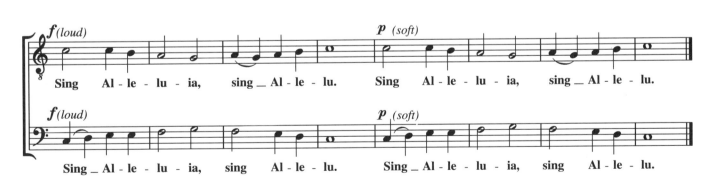

MIXED CHORUS

Winter

For SATB a cappella

TENNYSON (Adapted)

Music by
EMILY CROCKER

MIXED CHORUS

POSTURE/BREATH

1. Stretch your arms overhead, then bend at the waist and stretch toward the floor. Slowly rise up, one vertebra at a time until you are in a standing posture.

2. Rotate your shoulders, first your left, then your right, then both shoulders. Raise your head so that it is in line with the spinal column, and not tilted up or down. Remember to stand in a good singing posture:
    *   Stand with feet apart (Is your weight balanced?)
    *   Knees unlocked (Can you bend them easily?)
    *   Back straight (Are you standing erect comfortably and not stiff?)
    *   Head erect (Is your chin level, and not too far up or down?)
    *   Rib cage lifted (Is your chest high and able to expand?)
    *   Shoulders relaxed (Are they comfortably down, not too far forward or back?)
    *   Hands at your side (Are they relaxed and free of tension?)

Holding Music: When you are singing your warm-up or performing a piece by memory, your hands should be at your sides. This position allows you to practice full, deep breathing without restriction.

When you are holding a folder or music in your hands, hold the music up, so that your head is erect and lined with the spine. This also allows you to watch the conductor. By keeping your elbows up and your arms away from your body, you allow your rib cage to be expanded, and full deep breathing to occur.

It's always best for each singer to have his/her own copy of music. Sometimes, however, this is not possible, and two or more singers have to share music. When this is the case, try to maintain a good singing posture. Hold the music up and out from the body, and if necessary turn slightly so that you are both facing the direction of the conductor.

ARTICULATION

We have concentrated on vowel sound so far (ee, eh, ah, oh, oo). The sung word in music requires articulation to produce the consonants. The articulators that we use in vocal music are the teeth, the lips and the tongue.

3. For practice, repeat this short phrase quickly and precisely, concentrating on clean and clear articulation:

    The lips, the teeth, the tip of the tongue...the lips, the teeth, the tip of the tongue... (etc.)

ARTICULATION

For each of the following exercises remember to:
- Take a full, expanded rib cage breath before each repetition.
- Sing pure vowels with a relaxed jaw and vertical space inside your mouth.
- Articulate all the consonants so they are clear and precise.
- Sing both consonants and vowels with the same breath support.
- Repeat at different pitch levels, both higher and lower.
- A fermata (⌒) over a note means to hold the note longer than its normal value.

④

⑤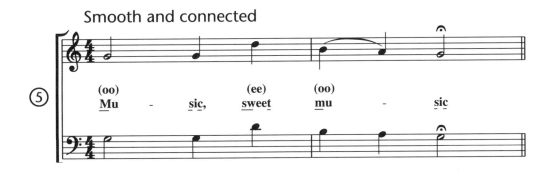

⑥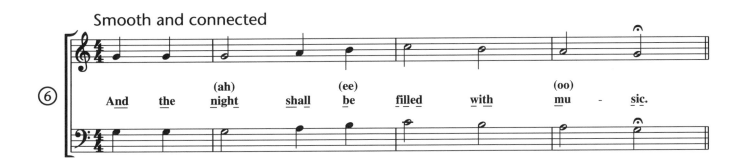

SHARPS & FLATS • REVIEW OF C MAJOR

You'll recall the order of whole/half steps for the C major scale:

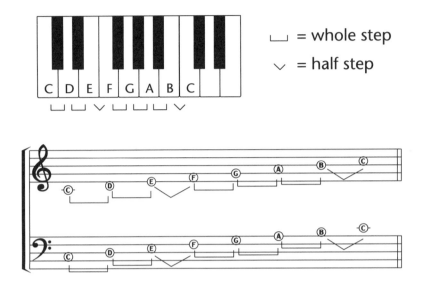

Music may be written with any note being the keynote. Because the order of whole/half steps must always be followed regardless of the keynote, the need arises for *sharps* (♯) and *flats* (♭).

A *sharp* raises the pitch one half step. This note, F♯ (F sharp), would be written with the sharp sign to the left of the notehead.

A *flat* lowers the pitch one half step. This note B♭ (B flat), would be written with the flat sign to the left of the notehead.

Practice
Name the following pitches:

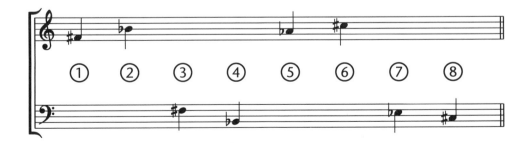

SHARPS & FLATS • KEY OF G MAJOR

To build a major scale starting on G, using the same arrangement of whole steps and half steps as in the key of C major, you'll notice the need for an F#.

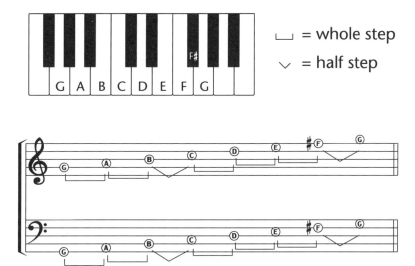

⌐⌐ = whole step

∨ = half step

If we had written F - G, the *interval* (distance) between these two pitches would have been a whole step rather than the required half step.

Check your knowledge!
1. What is the order of whole/half steps for any major scale?
2. Does a *sharp* raise or lower a pitch? By how much?
3. Does a *flat* raise or lower a pitch? By how much?

Key of G Practice
Practice singing the key of G scale. Three octaves of the G scale are written below. Because of the wider range, you'll only be able to sing a portion of the three *octaves*, but take note of your own vocal range. What is your lowest note? Your highest note?

Remember that middle C can be written on its own little line in either clef. Other pitches may be written that way also. These little lines are called *ledger lines*. Ledger lines may be used to represent notes either above or below the staff.

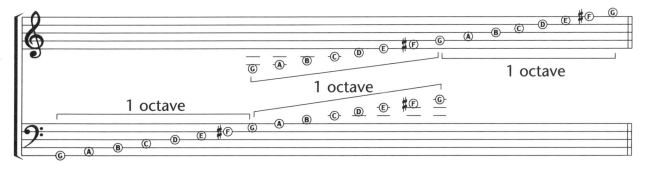

KEY OF G PRACTICE

Identify the following pitches in the key of G. Echo-sing or sing as a group.

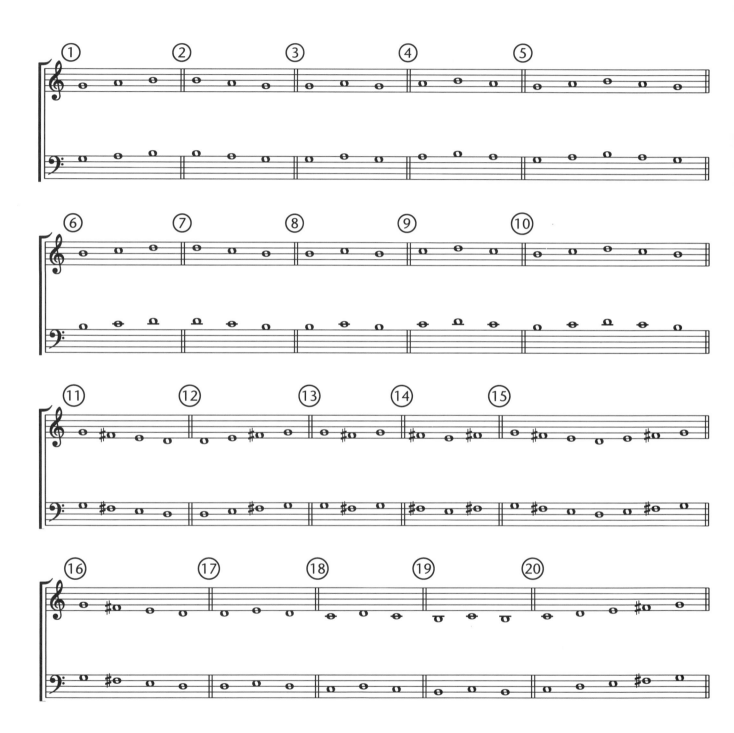

KEY OF G PRACTICE

Sing each line separately and in any combination.

MUSICAL TERMS

mf - *mezzo forte*, medium loud

mp - *mezzo piano*, medium soft

legato - smooth and connected. Sometimes indicated by placing the word *legato* above the staff or at the beginning of the song or section of a song. Also indicated by a *slur* above the notes to be performed legato.

From "Erin" for **Treble Chorus** on p. 59.

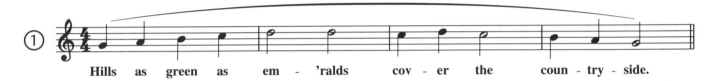

From "Sing Your Songs" for **Mixed Chorus** on p. 61.

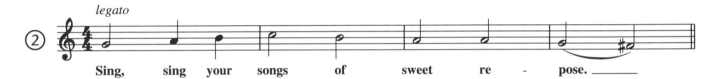

staccato - notes are to be performed short and detached. Usually written by placing a dot above or below the notehead:

From "Shipwrecked" for **Tenor Bass** Chorus on p. 60.

style marking - a word or phrase placed at the beginning of a song or section of a song to indicate in general, the way the piece should be performed. Sometimes style markings also include a *metronome marking* (♩ = 108) to indicate the tempo. This means 108 metronome beats per minute.

Identify the style markings for "Erin," "Sing Your Songs," and "Shipwrecked."

TREBLE CHORUS

Erin

For SA a cappella

Traditional Irish (adapted)

**Music by
EMILY CROCKER**

TENOR BASS CHORUS

Shipwrecked!

For TB a cappella

Traditional (adapted)

Music by EMILY CROCKER

MIXED CHORUS

Sing Your Songs

For SATB a cappella

Words and Music by
JOHN LEAVITT

Peacefully, legato (♩ = 112)

POSTURE/BREATH/TONE

1. Lift the left shoulder high and then let it fall. Repeat with the right shoulder and then both shoulders. Drop the head to the chest gently and then let it roll to the right and then the left. Stretch overhead, fall forward like a rag doll and then gradually stand up to a good singing posture.

2. Imagine a balloon is attached to the top of your head. Allow it to lift your head until it is in alignment with your spine and your rib cage is lifted.

3. Sniff in air 2 times quickly, then puff out 2 times quickly.
   Sniff 3, puff 3
   Sniff 4, puff 4
   Sniff 4, puff 2
   Sniff 2, puff 4

   Notice how the air in your lungs feels buoyant. Try to maintain this buoyant feeling of breath support as you sing the following vocalises.

Tone/Articulation: In each of the following exercises remember to:
- Maintain a good singing posture.
- Take a full expanded rib cage breath before each repetition.
- Activate the *articulators* (lips, teeth, tongue).
- Produce good tone by concentrating on vowel formation and vertical space inside the mouth.
- Repeat at different pitch levels, both higher and lower.

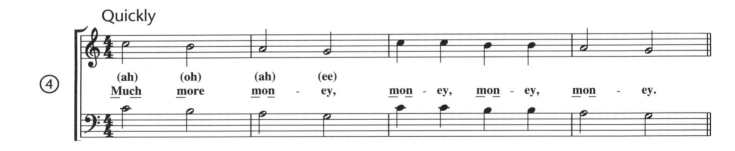

ARTICULATION

This exercise concentrates on "tip-of-the-tongue" consonants. Sing it quickly, lightly, and without a lot of jaw movement.

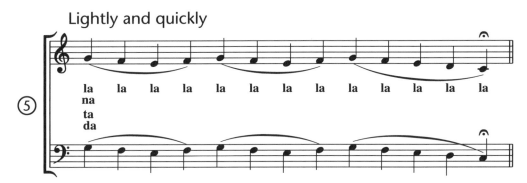

In the following exercise the "st" sounds of "first" and "star" should merge together to maintain a smooth legato phrase.

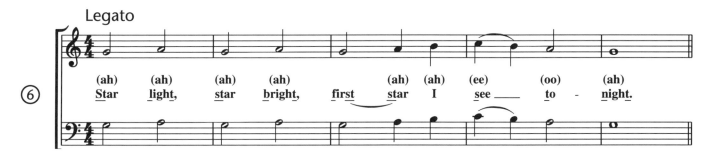

Never prolong the "s" into a hiss. Move quickly on to the next vowel or consonant.

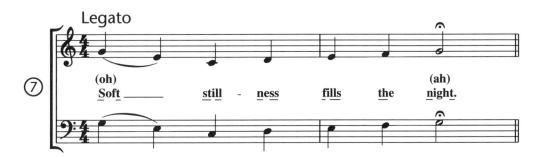

ACCIDENTALS · KEY SIGNATURE

Let's review sharps and flats.

A *sharp* raises the pitch one half step. This note, F♯ (F sharp), would be written with the sharp sign to the left of the notehead.

A *flat* lowers the pitch one half step. This note B♭ (B flat), would be written with the flat sign to the left of the notehead.

There are two ways to write sharps and flats in music. One way is to write the sharp or flat to the left of the notehead as shown above. These are called *accidentals* because they are not normally found in the key in which you are performing.

The other way is to write a *key signature.* Since we know that the key of G will always use an F♯, rather than write the sharp sign on every F in the song, we simply write a sharp on F's line at the beginning of the song right after the clef sign(s) and before the time signature. (Note: The key signature is used with every clef sign in the song as a reminder.)

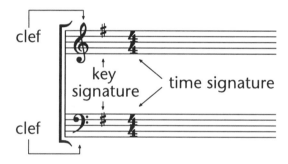

Placing an F♯ in the key signature indicates that the music is in the key of *G major* which always uses an F♯. Remember that the key of *C major* has no sharps or flats. Thus, the absence of sharps or flats in the key signature indicates that the music is in the key of C major.

Check your knowledge!

1. What is an *accidental?*

2. Where is a *sharp* or *flat* sign placed for a single note?

3. Where is a *key signature* placed?

4. What is the key signature for C major? For G major?

KEY OF G PRACTICE

Sing notes and steps as indicated.

MORE KEY OF G PRACTICE

Sing each line separately and in any combination. Notice that not every melody starts on the keynote G. Identify the starting pitch of each melody and sing up or down the scale to locate the starting pitch.

TREBLE • TENOR BASS • MIXED

Musical Terms

tempo - speed of the beat

rit. - from the Italian *ritardando*, meaning gradually slower. When you see this term in music the *tempo* or speed of the beat gradually slows.

a tempo - from the Italian "to the time" meaning to return to the original tempo; often used after a *ritardando*.

—————————— - a symbol meaning *crescendo*, or gradually louder.

—————————— - the reverse of the above, *decrescendo*, or *diminuendo*, meaning gradually softer.

‖: :‖ repeat sign; repeat the section. If the first repeat sign is omitted, go back to the very beginning.

Music History

A *canon* is a musical form in which a melody in one part is followed a short time later by other parts performing the same melody. Sometimes the difference in time is as short as 1 beat, other times it may be several measures. Canons are sometimes called *rounds*, and you may know several already: "Row, Row, Row Your Boat," "Are You Sleeping," etc.

Canons are interesting musical forms because the *melody*, entering at staggered intervals produces *harmony*, when several voices are combined. This combination of voices in music is sometimes called texture. The earliest known canon dates to the 13th century and is called *Sumer is icumen in* ("Summer is a-coming in")

In the Middle Ages, a small place of worship was called a *cappella*, meaning "chapel". Later, the musicians (originally called the *schola*) who sang in these chapels became known as the *cappella*. After 1600 *a cappella* took on its present meaning, which is to sing unaccompanied by instruments.

JOYFULLY SING

Joyfully Sing, on p. 68 is a canon. As you learn this canon follow this procedure:
• Chant the rhythm of the unison melody, then add pitch. Repeat as needed to become secure. Add the text.
• Combine the three parts as a canon. After all three parts have sung the complete canon melody sing the ending.
• Sing musically with dynamics, good tone quality, and expression.

Joyfully Sing

For 3-Part a cappella

Words and Music by
EMILY CROCKER

POSTURE/BREATH

Posture: Check your posture and ask yourself these questions.
- Stand with feet apart (Is your weight balanced?)
- Knees unlocked (Can you bend them easily?)
- Back straight (Are you standing erect comfortably and not stiff?)
- Head erect (Is your chin level, and not too far up or down?)
- Rib cage lifted (Is your chest high and able to expand?)
- Shoulders relaxed (Are they comfortably down, not too far forward or back?)
- Hands at your side (Are they relaxed and free of tension?)

Coordinated Breathing
When you swing a bat or throw a ball, you use preparation, attack, and follow-through. It's the same with singing:

Inhalation - is your preparation. Just like the backswing of the racket, you must judge the distance, length and the loudness of the phrase you will sing.

Exhalation - Just like throwing a ball (attack), this is the part of breathing that requires the most coordination. When you throw a ball, your strength, knowledge, technical precision and discipline affect your accuracy. It's the same in breathing. The more you know, the more you've practiced, and the amount of effort you apply all combine to help you sing with a fully supported tone.

Release - As you end a musical phrase, follow-through with the breath for a pleasing and accurate release. Just as you wouldn't choke your baseball swing, don't choke off the breath at the end of a phrase. When you release a phrase well, you also prepare for the next breath.

1. Breathe through an imaginary straw. Feel the expansion in your rib cage as your lungs fill with air. Sing the following pattern, and as you release the tone, also exhale the rest of your air. Repeat at different pitch levels.

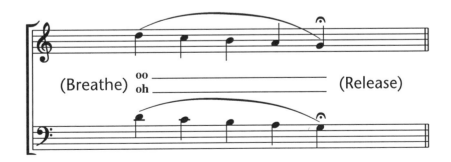

The Breathing Process

The physical aspect of breathing involves several different parts of the body.

During inhalation, the *diaphragm* muscle contracts, flattens and moves downward toward the feet. This motion pushes against the abdomen, pushing it outward. At the same time, the *intercostal muscles* (rib muscles) also contract, moving the ribs outward, expanding the rib cage. Since the lungs are attached to the diaphragm and the ribs, the lungs expand, and air rushes in.

When you sing, your exhalation is controlled, the abdominal muscles contract and the ribs stay expanded to provide resistance and control to the exhalation.

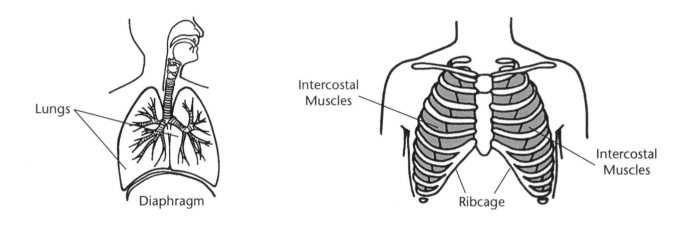

2. As you sing the following exercise, remember to:
   • Take a full expanded rib cage breath, remembering "prepare, attack, and follow-through" as you inhale, exhale on a tone, and release.
   • Breathe "on the vowel," i.e., if you are to sing an "ah," take your breath in an "ah" shape. This helps prepare you to sing with a relaxed jaw and vertical mouth space.

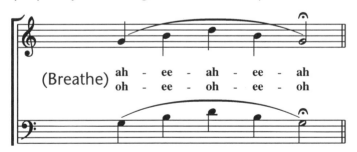

RESTS

Rests are silences in music. They come in a variety of lengths, just like notes. These silences are just as important as the notes.

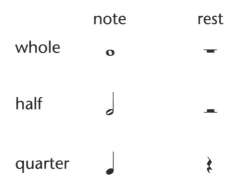

	note	rest
whole	o	—
half	♩	—
quarter	♩	♪

Rests and notes of the same name share the same duration.

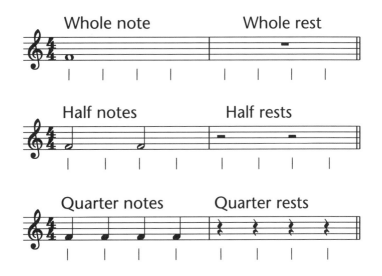

Check your knowledge!

1. Define *rests* in music.

2. Identify the following rests: ▬   ↕   ▬

3. In $\frac{4}{4}$ meter, how many beats does a whole rest receive? A half rest? A quarter rest?

 PRACTICE WITH RESTS

Read each line (clap, tap, or chant)

Animal Song

For 4-Part Speech Chorus

Divide the choir into any number of groups up to four. Each group may chant one of the four numbered parts. Each part may proceed to the next part sequentially without break in rhythm. (example: group 1 sings parts 1-2-3-4, group 2 sings parts 2-3-4-1, etc.) Work for a sing-song kind of inflected speech at a light dynamic level. Practice slowly at first and gradually increase the speed of the beat.

Traditional Lyrics

Music by
JOHN LEAVITT

Quick inflected speech, lightly

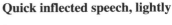

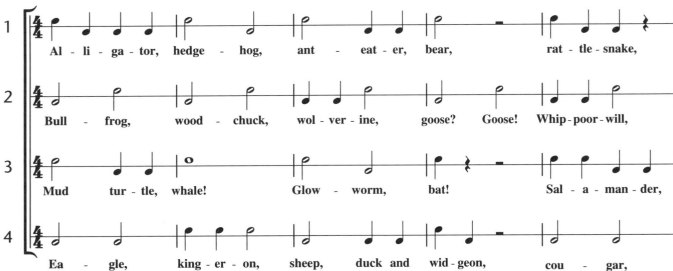

1. Al - li - ga - tor, hedge - hog, ant - eat - er, bear, rat - tle - snake,
2. Bull - frog, wood - chuck, wol - ver - ine, goose? Goose! Whip - poor - will,
3. Mud tur - tle, whale! Glow - worm, bat! Sal - a - man - der,
4. Ea - gle, king - er - on, sheep, duck and wid - geon, cou - gar,

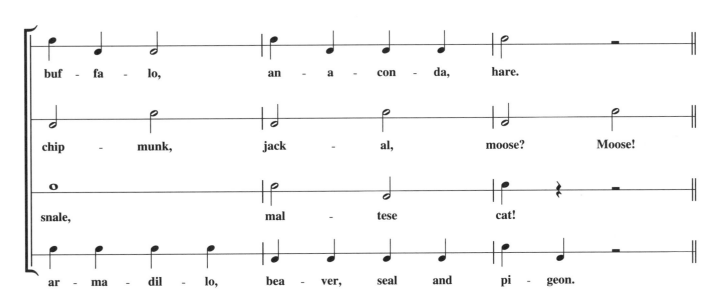

buf - fa - lo, an - a - con - da, hare.
chip - munk, jack - al, moose? Moose!
snale, mal - tese cat!
ar - ma - dil - lo, bea - ver, seal and pi - geon.

 REVIEW AND PRACTICE

Answer the following questions orally in large or small group discussion. Refer to previous chapters as needed.

1. Describe the steps for a good singing posture.

2. Why is good posture important in singing?

3. Describe a good singing posture for singing from memory. Describe a good singing posture for holding music. For sharing music with another singer.

4. What are the *five basic vowels* used in singing?

5. Why do we need *articulation* in singing?

6. What are the *articulators*?

7. What are the three stages of breathing for singing?

8. Describe the action of the *diaphragm* during breathing. The abdomen. The ribs. The lungs.

Tone/Articulation

Review all the elements of good singing in the following exercise:

- Take a full expanded rib cage breath, maintain the support while singing the phrase, and release.
- Breathe with your mouth in the shape of the vowel you are preparing to sing.
- Repeat at different pitch levels, both higher and lower.

Text by William Blake

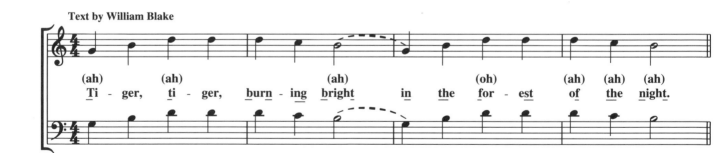

(ah) (ah) (ah) (oh) (ah) (ah) (ah)
Ti - ger, ti - ger, burn - ing bright in the for - est of the night.

REVIEW AND PRACTICE

Check your knowledge!

1. Name the order of whole steps and half steps for any major scale.

2. Define *sharp*. Define *flat*.

3. Name two ways sharps and flats can be placed in music.

4. Where is a sharp or flat sign placed in relation to the notehead.

5. Where is a *key signature* placed?

6. Name the key signature for C major. For G major.

7. What is the term for silences in music?

8. Identify the following rests:

9. How many quarter rests equal a half rest? How many half rests equal a whole note?

10. In $\frac{4}{4}$ meter, how many beats are in two whole notes?

Matching Drill

①   a) whole step

②   b) quarter rests

③   c) G major

④   d) half step

⑤   e) C major

⑥   f) F sharp

⑦   g) B flat

⑧   h) half rests

KEY OF G • RESTS

Sing each line separately and in any combination.

①

②

③

④

⑤

⑥

⑦

⑧

UNISON VOICES

Music History: The text for this short piece was written by the Scottish poet Robert Louis Stevenson and included in his collection of poems for children: *A Child's Garden of Verses.* Stevenson, who lived from 1850-1894, also wrote two of the most famous novels ever written, *Treasure Island* and *The Strange Case of Dr. Jekyll and Mr. Hyde.*

Rain
For Unison voices and Piano

ROBERT LOUIS STEVENSON

Music by
EMILY CROCKER

POSTURE/BREATH

1. Stretch high overhead. Bend at the waist and gradually stand upright, one vertebra at a time. Nod your head "yes" several times, then "no."

2. Yawn-sigh

3. Imagine there is a milkshake as large as the room. "Drink" the air through a large straw. Exhale on a yawn-sigh.

4. Sip in air as though you were sipping water. Notice the cool feeling in your throat.

5. Breathe in with your lips in an "oo" shape, then sing the following exercise. Repeat the pattern at different pitch levels, both higher and lower. Open the vowel to an "ah" as you go higher and an "oh" as you go lower.

(Breathe on "oo") "oo"   (breathe) *etc.*

6. Take a full, relaxed breath and sing on a staccato "hoo."

Short and detached

hoo   hoo   hoo   hoo   hoo

These exercises, and many others you will learn, contribute toward a relaxed and *open throat*. An open throat will help you produce a free, open tone that is not constricted or tension-filled, and will help keep your voice healthy. This is important as you develop resonance and flexibility in your voice.

Vocalization

The source of vocal tone is the *larynx* (pronounced "LEH-rinks" and popularly called the "voice box"). The larynx is a part of the *respiratory system* and is not muscle, but is made of *cartilage*. The larynx is located midway between the mouth, nose and throat above, and the lungs and *trachea* (air passages) below.

You can find your own larynx by locating your "Adam's Apple." If your Adam's apple is not prominent, you can feel it if you lightly run your fingertip down the front of your neck from your chin, until you feel a hard structure with a sharp upper edge. If you hold your finger here while you say "ah" you can feel the vibration that the larynx produces.

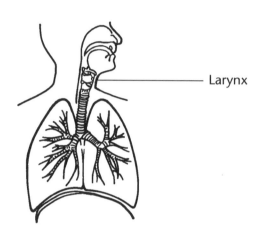

The Vocal Folds

The *vocal folds* (also called *vocal cords*) are a pair of muscles attached to the front and back of the larynx. They open and close somewhat like a valve – open for breathing, closed for singing (and speaking). Exhaled air passes between the gently closed vocal folds, causing them to vibrate. The number of vibrations per second produces pitch. The following illustration shows the vocal folds from above.

The Vocal Folds (seen from above)

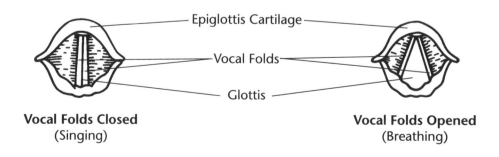

80

MELODIC INTERVALS

An *interval* is the measurement of distance between two pitches. When intervals are played in succession, they are called *melodic intervals*. Following are examples of intervals of 2nds, 3rds, 4ths, and 5ths.

Read the pitches, echo sing, or sing each example as a group:

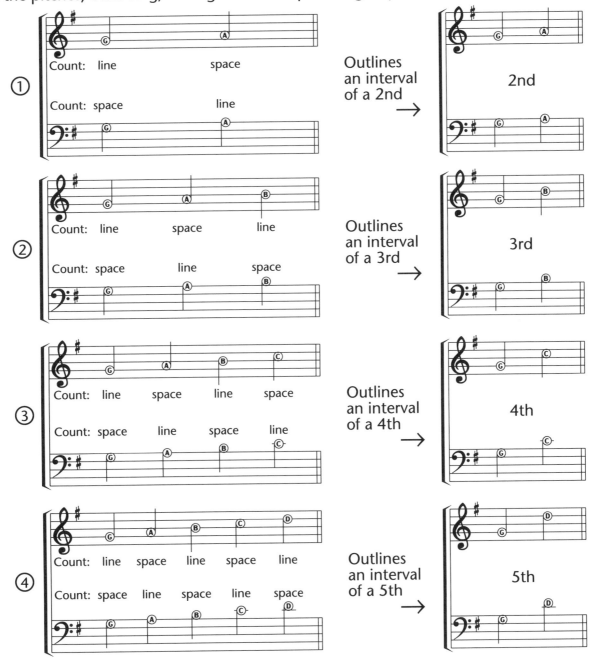

Check your knowledge!

1. What is an *interval*?

MELODIC INTERVAL PRACTICE

Identify the following intervals.

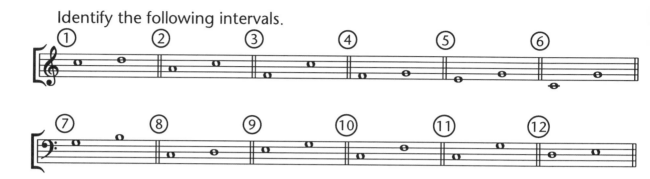

Sing the following interval drills.

13   C   D, that's a sec-ond, C   E, that's a third, C   F, that's a fourth, C   G, that's a fifth,

G   C, that's a fifth, F   C, that's a fourth, E   C, that's a third, D   C, that's a sec-ond.

14   G   A, that's a sec-ond, G   B, that's a third, G   C, that's a fourth, G   D, that's a fifth,

D   G, that's a fifth, C   G, that's a fourth, B   G, that's a third, A   G, that's a sec-ond.

KEY OF C INTERVAL PRACTICE

Practice the following exercises. Echo sing, or sing as a group.

KEY OF G INTERVAL PRACTICE

Practice the following exercises. Echo sing, or sing as a group.

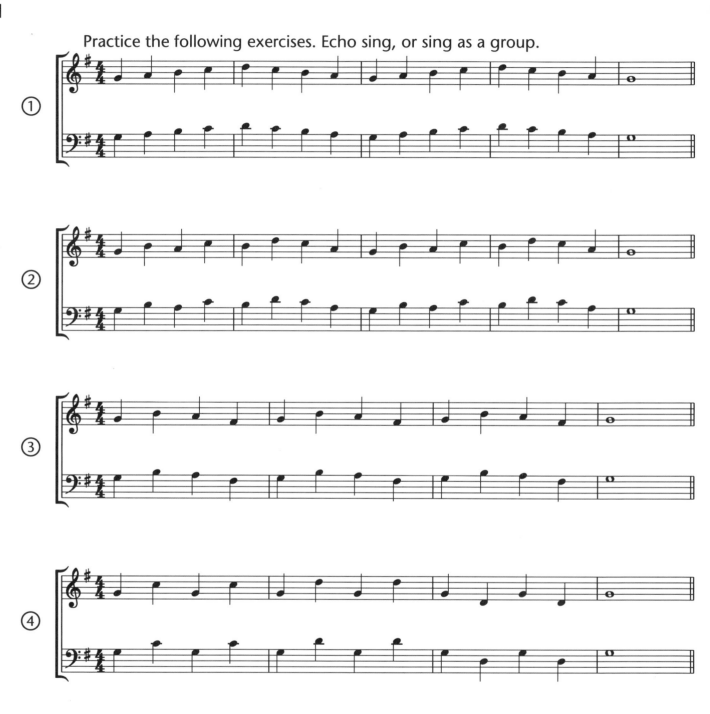

TREBLE CHORUS

Sing Hosanna

For SA a cappella

TENOR BASS CHORUS

Sing Hosanna

For TB a cappella

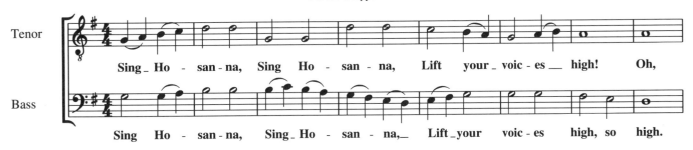

MIXED CHORUS

Sing Hosanna

For SATB a cappella

POSTURE/BREATH

1. Stretch overhead, side to side, up and down, then shake to relax any tight muscles.

2. Raise your arms overhead, stretching the fingers out in all directions. Bring the arms back to the sides, relaxed and free of tension.

3. Exhale all your air. Wait for a moment until your body lets you know it needs air. Allow the air to flow in without effort.

4. Sip air through a straw. Allow your lungs and rib cage to expand outward.

5. Place your fingertips just below your rib cage and take a "surprised" breath. Notice the movement of the diaphragm.

Tone

Review the 5 basic vowels used in choral singing: ee, eh, ah, oh, oo. Remember when you sing these vowels to sing with a relaxed jaw and vertical space inside the mouth.

ee   eh   ah   oh   oo

TONE

There are many other vowel sounds used in both speaking and singing. Here are some examples of other vowel sounds. As a general rule: Sing the vowel sound as you would say it, but modify the vowel in the following ways:

- Keep a relaxed jaw
- Maintain vertical space inside the mouth
- Keep the corners of the mouth from spreading outward

Repeat ⑦ - ⑨ at different pitch levels

⑦ (ih)   (ih)   (ih)   (ih)
Bring a gift of silk to the la - dy.

"ĭ" as in <u>gift</u>

⑧ (ă)   (ă)   (ă)
The cat sat in the hat.

"ă" as in <u>cat</u>

⑨ (ŭ)   (ŭ)
Fun _____ in the sun

"ŭ" as in <u>fun</u>

HARMONIC INTERVALS

Let's review intervals. In the last chapter we learned that an *interval* is the measurement between two pitches. When intervals are played in succession, they are called *melodic intervals*.

When intervals are played simultaneously, they are called *harmonic* intervals. Here are some examples of harmonic intervals.

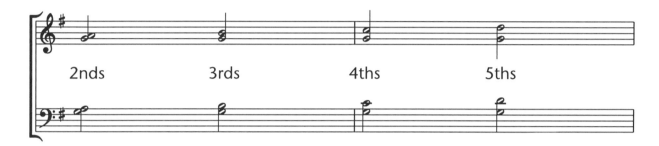

2nds   3rds   4ths   5ths

Harmonic intervals are the building blocks of harmony. Two or more harmonic intervals combined form a *chord*. Thus, a *chord* is the combination of 3 or more tones played simultaneously. Here are some examples of chords.

Check your knowledge!
1. What are intervals played simultaneously called?

2. What are intervals played in succession called?

3. What is a *chord*?

PRACTICE WITH INTERVALS

Practice the following exercises. Notice the harmonic intervals that result when one group sustains a pitch while the other group moves to a higher or lower pitch. Listen carefully for balance, tuning, and blend.

Remember that a fermata (𝄐) means to hold a note (or rest) longer than its normal value.

Practice the following exercises in 3 parts. Notice the chord that results as one group sustains a pitch while 2 other groups move higher and lower.

MELODY AND HARMONY

Sing each line separately and in combination. Can you describe the time and key signature?

TREBLE • TENOR BASS • MIXED

Musical Terms

accent; emphasis on one note (or chord) over others around it. When singing a note that is accented, you can emphasize the note by singing it louder or by stressing the beginning consonant or vowel that starts the word. You can also use the diaphragm to create a breath accent.

accel. – accelerando; becoming faster; a gradual increase in tempo.

History: The author of this text, *Francis Beaumont*, was an English playwright who lived from c.1584-1616 and was a contemporary of William Shakespeare. It was quite common for plays of this period to use music.

Dance!

For SA, TB or SATB and Piano

Text by
FRANCIS BEAUMONT (1584-1616)

Music by
EMILY CROCKER

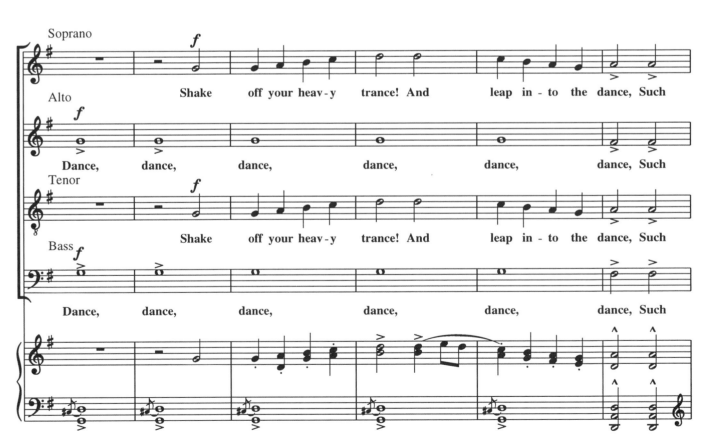

POSTURE/BREATH

1. Stretch your arms overhead, then bend at the waist and stretch toward the floor. Slowly rise up, one vertebra at a time until you are in a standing posture.

2. Rotate your shoulders, first your left, then your right, then both shoulders. Raise your head so that it is in line with the spinal column, and not tilted up or down. Remember to stand in a good singing posture:
   - Stand with feet apart (Is your weight balanced?)
   - Knees unlocked (Can you bend them easily?)
   - Back straight (Are you standing erect comfortably and not stiff?)
   - Head erect (Is your chin level, and not too far up or down?)
   - Rib cage lifted (Is your chest high and able to expand?)
   - Shoulders relaxed (Are they comfortably down, not too far forward or back?)
   - Hands at your side (Are they relaxed and free of tension?)

3. When people are suddenly startled, they usually take a deep natural breath very quickly. Take a "surprised" breath. Notice the action of the diaphragm.

4. Imagine that there is an elevator platform at the bottom of your lungs. Drop the platform toward the floor as you inhale. Inhale 4 counts, exhale 4 counts. Repeat with 5, then 6 counts.

Physical Exercise: A regular program of physical exercise is very useful in a singer's development. Exercise improves breath capacity, the cardiovascular system, endurance, and general good health. Be sure to have a physician's approval before beginning any exercise program, but the benefits of such a program are significant.

Tone/Articulation
Review the following vowels: ĭ (gift), ă (cat), ŭ (run)

THE NEUTRAL VOWEL

The second syllable of the following words and several one-syllable words use what is called the neutral vowel (ə), also called *schwa*. It might be described as similar to an "uh" sound, and is an unstressed word or syllable. To produce this vowel:

- Keep space inside the mouth
- Maintain a vertical mouth shape
- Do not allow the corners of the mouth to spread outward
- The mouth is more closed than an "ah" vowel

Examples:

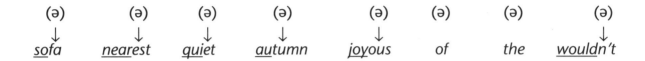

(ə)	(ə)	(ə)	(ə)	(ə)	(ə)	(ə)	(ə)
↓	↓	↓	↓	↓			↓
s*o*fa	n*ea*rest	qui*e*t	*au*tumn	j*o*yous	of	the	w*ou*ldn't

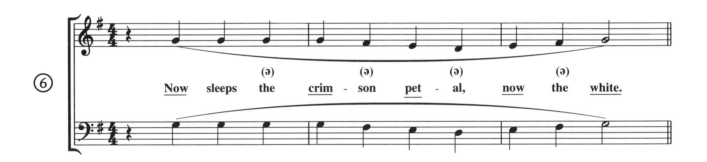

⑥ Now sleeps the crim - son pet - al, now the white.

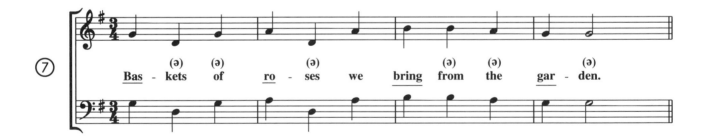

⑦ Bas - kets of ro - ses we bring from the gar - den.

TRIAD AND TONIC CHORD

Let's review chords. In the last chapter, we learned that two or more harmonic intervals combined form a *chord*. So, a *chord* is the combination of 3 or more tones played or sung simultaneously.

A *triad* is a special type of 3-note chord built in 3rds over a *root tone*. Following are some examples of triads.

When a *triad* is built on the key note of a major scale it is called a *tonic chord*. You'll notice that the word *tonic* is related to the word tone. *Tonic* is another way of referring to the keynote in a major scale and *tonic chord* is another way of referring to the triad built on that keynote.

Check your knowledge!

1. How many tones are needed to form a chord?

2. Describe a *triad*.

3. What is another name for keynote?

4. What tone of the major scale is a tonic chord built on?

5. Is the *tonic chord* a triad?

TONIC CHORD PRACTICE

Practice the following drills which outline the tonic chord. Remember, when the melody outlines the tonic chord, you are singing melodic intervals. When 3 or more parts sing the pitches of the tonic chord simultaneously, the ensemble is singing a chord.

The Tonic Chord

Melody Drills

Chord Builders

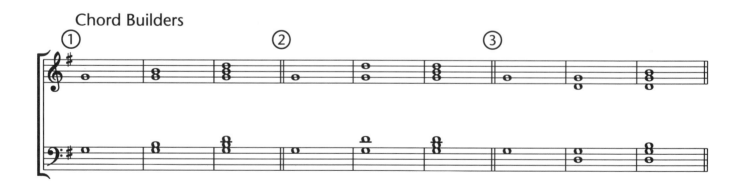

 MORE TONIC CHORD PRACTICE

Echo-sing each line or sing as a group, until the melodic patterns of the tonic chord are familiar.

TONIC CHORD EXERCISES

Sing each line separately and in any combination.

TREBLE CHORUS

History: In this piece for treble chorus, the text is by Christina Rossetti, a 19th century English poet who lived in the Victorian era from 1830-1894. Rossetti, who has been described as one of the greatest poets of her time, wrote both of nature and of the spirit. Her brother, Dante Gabriel Rossetti, was also a well-known poet and painter.

Musical Terms:

opt. div. – optional *divisi*; the part splits into optional harmony. The smaller sized *cue notes* indicate the optional notes to be used.

As you prepare *Spring Quiet*, concentrate on the following:
- Notice the interval skips in the *tonic chord*.
- In measures 9 and 11, notice the quarter rest on the first beat of the measure.
- In measure 17, the melody is presented as a *canon*. In measure 21, notice how the melody outlines the *tonic chord*.
- Sing with full breath support and good vowels and articulation.
- If you sing the *opt. divisi*, notice the full 3-part tonic chord in the last measure.

Spring Quiet

For SA a cappella

CHRISTINA ROSSETTI (adapted)

Music by
EMILY CROCKER

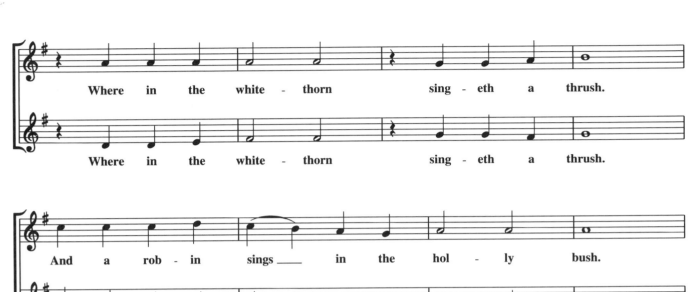

Where in the white - thorn sing - eth a thrush.

Where in the white - thorn sing - eth a thrush.

And a rob - in sings ___ in the hol - ly bush.

And a rob - in sings ___ in the hol - ly bush.

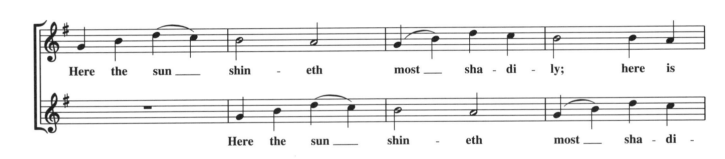

Here the sun ___ shin - eth most ___ sha - di - ly; here is

Here the sun ___ shin - eth most ___ sha - di -

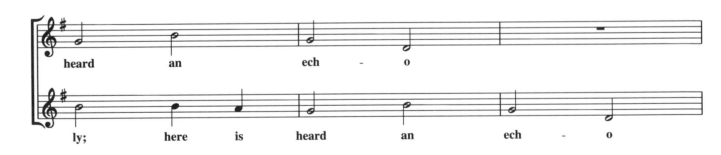

heard an ech - o

ly; here is heard an ech - o

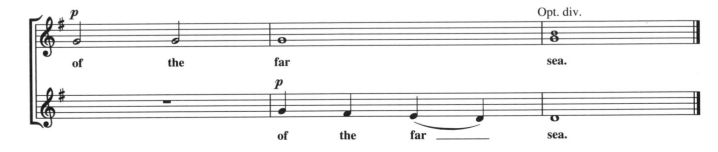

of the far sea.

of the far ___ sea.

TENOR BASS CHORUS

History: In music during the 16th century, an *ode* was a text set to music in a strict chordal style and in a rhythm dictated by the rhythm of the words of the poem.

The text for the piece that follows, *Sons of Art*, while contemporary, has similarities to the odes of an earlier time.

Henry Purcell (1659-1695) was an English composer of the Baroque Period who wrote odes and hundreds of other songs, choral pieces, instrumental and dramatic works. As a composer for the English court, in 1694 he wrote a famous ode on the occasion of Queen Mary II's birthday entitled *Come Ye Sons of Art, Away*.

Musical Terms:

ostinato – a repeated pattern. Notice how the bass part in this piece repeats the same four bars. This serves as an accompaniment device beneath the tenor melody.

opt. div. – optional *divisi*; the part splits into optional harmony. The smaller sized *cue notes* indicate the optional notes to be used.

fine – an Italian term for *end*. After a repeat the *fine* sign indicates the end of the piece.

As you prepare *Sons of Art*:
- Use good breath support, vowels, and articulation.
- Sing musically.
- If you sing the *opt. divisi* at the end, notice the full 3-part tonic chord in the last measure.

Sons of Art

For TB a cappella

Words and Music by
EMILY CROCKER

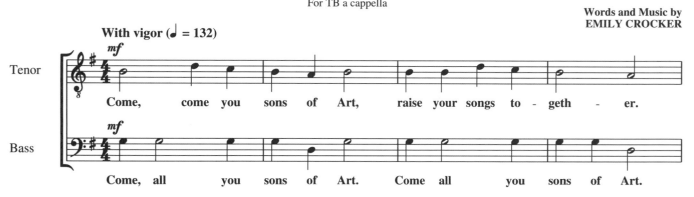

TENOR BASS

Mu - sic _____ mu - sic, all our tri - butes bring.

Mu - sic, mu - sic, all our tri - butes bring.

Mu - sic, mu - sic, our hearts and voic - es sing.

Mu - sic, mu - sic, our hearts _ and voic - es sing.

Come, come you sons of Art, join the hap - py cho - rus.

Come, all you sons of Art. Come all you sons of Art.

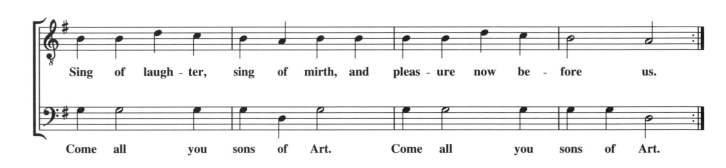

Sing of laugh - ter, sing of mirth, and pleas - ure now be - fore us.

Come all you sons of Art. Come all you sons of Art.

MIXED CHORUS

History: In the early stages of America's nationhood, the purpose of education was aimed at practical and religious matters. Music for worship and recreation was primarily an oral tradition – people learned music by listening to it.

As time passed, however, the quality of singing declined so that a clergyman of the time wrote: "The tunes are now miserably tortured and twisted... into a horrid medley of confused and disordered voices."

In response to these concerns, *Singing Schools* developed. These singing schools were led by traveling teachers who for a fee would teach the basics of reading music in small towns and villages. Sometimes whole families would attend, and enjoyed the social aspect of singing together in a group.

Music became a part of the school curriculum for the first time in 1838 when *Lowell Mason* convinced the Boston School Committee to include it in the public schools.

Lowell Mason wrote many songs and choral pieces during his lifetime, including the text for the piece that follows.

As you prepare to sing *O Music, Sweet Music*:
• Notice how the melody outlines the tonic chord.
• When all three parts combine, listen as the 3-parts create harmony.
• In measure 9, the melody is restated, this time as a 3-part canon.
• Sing with good breath support, vowels, and articulation.

O Music, Sweet Music

For SATB a cappella

Words by LOWELL MASON
Music by JOHN LEAVITT

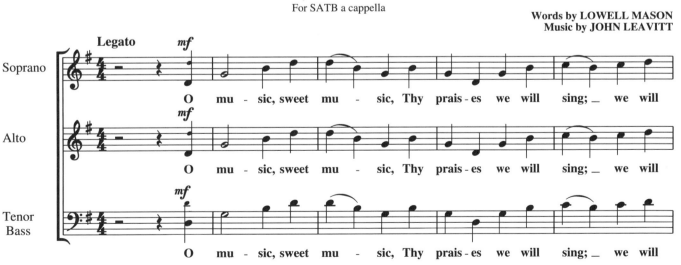

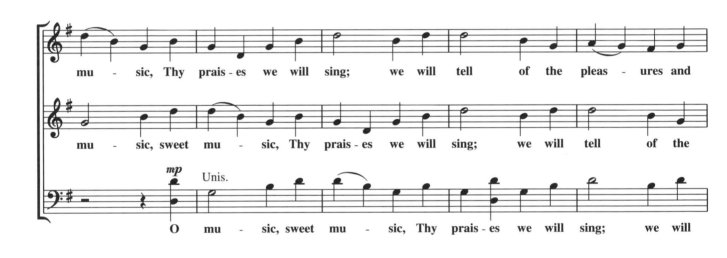

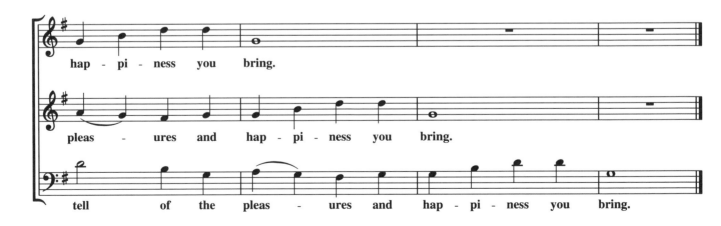

REVIEW AND PRACTICE

1.   Describe the steps for a good singing posture.

2.   How does an expanded rib cage affect breath capacity?

3.   What are the five basic vowel sounds? Describe the basic formation of each.

4.   What is the general rule for producing other vowel sounds in addition to the five basic vowel sounds?

5.   What is the *neutral vowel*?

6.   Describe the difference in the vowel sounds of the following:
     • 2nd syllable of *sofa*
     • 1st syllable of *father*

7.   What is *articulation* in singing? What are the three main *articulators*?

8.   What is the source of vocal tone? What is it popularly called?

9.   How do the vocal folds produce sound?

10. How can physical exercise help to improve singing?

Tone/Articulation

Sing the following exercise which reviews vowel shape and articulation. Repeat at different pitch levels.

In sweet mu - sic is such art kill - ing care and grief of heart.

REVIEW AND PRACTICE

Check your knowledge!

1. What is an *interval*?

2. What is the difference between *melodic* and *harmonic* intervals?

3. What is a *chord*?

4. How many tones are needed to form a chord?

5. What is the difference between a *chord* and a *triad*?

6. What is another name for *keynote*?

7. What tone of the major scale is a *tonic chord* built on?

8. Is the tonic chord a triad?

Identify the following melodic and harmonic intervals.

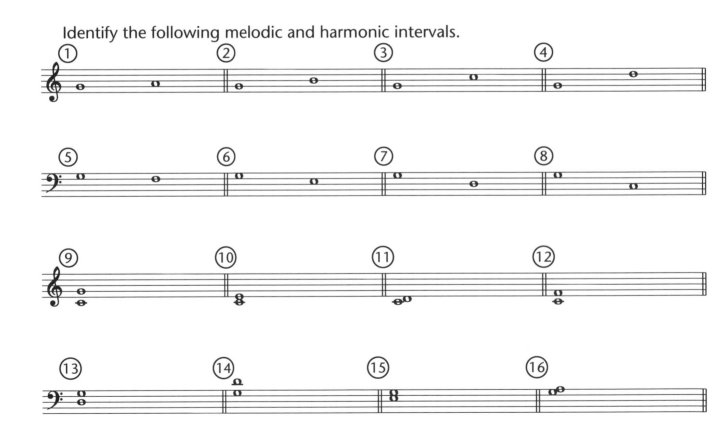

TONIC CHORD • PICKUP NOTE

Musical Terms:

pickup note(s) – A pickup note(s) (also called *upbeat* or *anacrusis*) is one or more notes which occur before the first barline.

Sing each line separately and in any combination. Notice the *pickup note* in each exercise.

KING WILLIAM
Treble Chorus • Tenor Bass Chorus

History: The text for *King William* is taken from an Early American *Play-Party* song. Play-parties were social events at which young people came together for refreshments, games, and singing. In many communities of the time, dancing was frowned upon, and while the play parties included ring dances, reels, and other partner games, the participants sang the songs without instrumental accompaniment, and so they were considered to be games or "play-parties" rather than actual dances.

In this play-party song, a young man would stand holding a broad-brimmed hat in his hand. Then he would place the hat on a girl's head, and they marched together, linking arms. At the end of the song, the girl placed the hat on another boy's head, and they continued as before. The song was repeated until all had a turn. At each "crowning" of the hat the couple would exchange a kiss.

As you prepare to perform *King William*:
- Find the places where the melody outlines the tonic chord. Practice these intervals so that you can sing them accurately.
- Read the rhythm, add the pitches, and repeat until accurate.
- Sing with good breath support and articulation.
- Identify the *neutral vowels* in the text and sing them with less stress:
  <u>Will</u>-iam   <u>Georg</u>-es, etc.

HOSANNA
Mixed Chorus

History: The word *Hosanna* (or *Osanna*) is a Hebrew word expressing triumph and glory. The phrase *Hosanna in excelsis Deo* is a phrase taken from the *Sanctus*, a section of the Latin mass. Since the advent of polyphony in music, the *Hosanna* has often been set to exciting music in a brilliant style. The *Hosanna* is often presented as a *coda* or ending section of the *Sanctus*.

As you prepare to perform *Hosanna*:
- Notice where the melody outlines the intervals of the tonic chord. Practice these sections so that you can sing them accurately.
- Notice how the parts enter in a staggered pattern, but not as in a canon. Rather, the entrances can be described as *imitative*, because they imitate each other, but not exactly.
- Read the rhythm, add the pitches, and repeat as necessary for accuracy.
- Pronounce the Latin phrases: *aw-SAH-nah een ek-SHEL-sees DEH-awh, Ah-leh-LOO-ee-ah.*
- Sing the last syllable of *Ho-SAN-na* as a neutral vowel.

TREBLE CHORUS

King William

For SA and Piano

Traditional text, adapted

Music by
EMILY CROCKER

TENOR BASS CHORUS

King William

For TB and Piano

Traditional text, adapted

Music by
EMILY CROCKER

Lyrics under the music:

one and all, cir - cle when you hear the call. Dance you all to

one and all, cir - cle when you hear the call. Dance you all to

fife and drum, cir - cle danc - ers one by one.

fife and drum, cir - cle danc - ers one by one.

MIXED CHORUS

Hosanna

For SATB and Piano

Music by
JOHN LEAVITT

POSTURE/BREATH/TONE

1. Stretch, then yawn-sigh.

2. As you stand in your best singing posture, concentrate on relaxing and releasing the tension in your body without slumping.
    *   Relax your neck and move your head forward and up, so that it is aligned with your spine.
    *   Allow your spinal column to lengthen vertically.
    *   Balance your weight evenly between your feet, and evenly between the heel and the ball of the feet.
    *   Release the tension in your knees.
    *   Release the tension in your shoulders.

3. Inhale with your mouth in an "ah" shape while pulling your elbows back. Bring your arms forward as you exhale on a whispered "oo." Repeat several times.

4. Imagine a milkshake as large as the room. "Drink" the air through a large straw.

Diphthongs (pronounced *DIF-thongs*)
You are familiar with the five basic vowels for choral singing: ee, eh, ah, oh, oo. As covered in previous chapters, other vowel sounds (ă, ŭ, ĭ, ə and others) are modifications of these basic vowels. A combination of two vowel sounds is called a *diphthong*. Since vowels are the basis of a free and open tone, and a choral sound that is blended and in tune, it is important to learn to sing vowels and diphthongs as an ensemble.

A diphthong consists of two vowel sounds: the *primary* vowel sound and a *secondary* vowel sound. This secondary vowel sound is (usually) at the very end of the diphthong, just before the final consonant or next word or syllable.

For example, the word "I" is really a diphthong using an "ah" and an "ee." The "ee" is a very brief, almost phantom sound at the end of the word.

I = ah _____ (ee)

ah

ee

DIPHTHONGS

Here are some other common diphthongs. Sing each word on a unison pitch, and concentrate on maintaining the pure, primary vowel sound. Just as you release, place the final secondary vowel sound at the end of the tone. It should be very understated and unstressed. Can you think of other examples? Can you find examples in the music you are rehearsing?

day = (d)eh _____ (ee)

joy = (j)aw _____ (ee)

though = (th)oh _____ (oo)

Some diphthongs are formed from consonant sounds, and the secondary sound occurs before the primary vowel sound:

you = (ee)oo _____

want = (oo)ah _____ (nt)

Practice the following exercises using diphthongs.

Repeat with:

youth (ee-<u>oo</u>-th)
wise (<u>oo</u>-<u>ah</u>-ee-z)

(5)

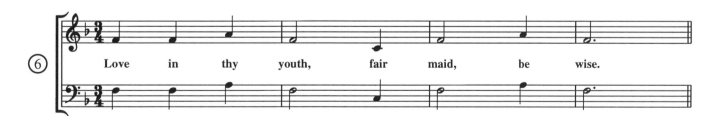

(6) Love in thy youth, fair maid, be wise.

DIPHTHONG PRACTICE

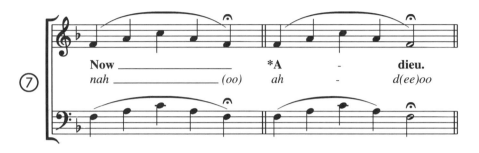

⑦ Now _____ *A - dieu.
nah _____ (oo) ah - d(ee)oo

Repeat with

my (m - <u>ah</u> - ee)
I (<u>ah</u> - ee)

* French for "good-bye"

⑧ Now un - to my la - dy

⑨ my _____
mah _____ (ee)

Repeat with

way (oo - <u>eh</u> - ee)
life (I - <u>ah</u> - ee -f)

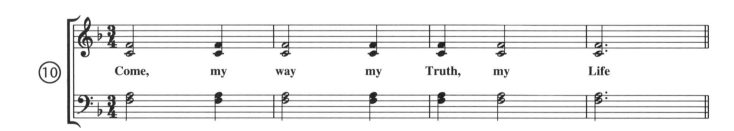

⑩ Come, my way my Truth, my Life

KEY OF F • DOTTED HALF NOTES

Key of F Major

The key of F major indicates that the keynote will be F. The grand staff below shows the F major scale as well as the whole/half step progression that is required for a major scale.

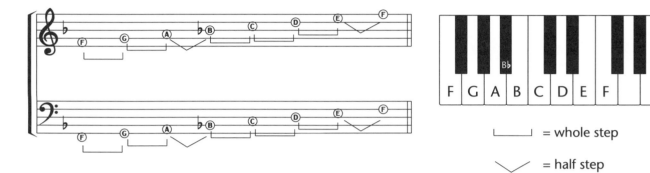

This time, the whole/half step progression requires a B flat. (Remember that a flat lowers a pitch by one half step.) If we had written A-B, the interval between these two pitches would have been a whole step rather than the required half step.

Remember also that a key signature is placed after the clef sign at the beginning of a line. This time the flat is on B's line, and indicates that every time B occurs in the music, it should be sung as a B flat.

Dotted half notes

In our music notation, we need to be able to measure note values with durations of three beats (especially in meters of 3). Our notational system accomplishes this by adding a dot to the right of a note head. The rule governing dotted notes is the dot receives *half the value of the note to which it is attached.*

$$\frac{3}{4} \quad \text{♩} \quad = \quad 2 \text{ beats} \qquad \frac{3}{4} \quad \text{♩.} \quad = \quad 3 \text{ beats}$$

Check your knowledge!

1. What is the key signature for the key of F major?

2. What is the dotted note rule?

3. How many beats does a half note receive in $\frac{3}{4}$ meter? A dotted half note?

KEY OF F • DOTTED HALF NOTES

The Tonic Chord   Chord–builder ①

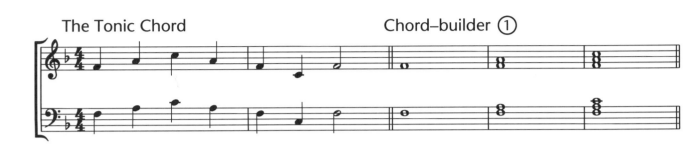

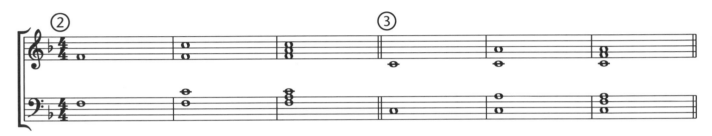

Chord Drill

Exercises in ¾

Sing each line separately and in any combination.

MORE PRACTICE

Sing each exercise separately and in any combination.

LOVE IN THY YOUTH
Treble Chorus

History: In the 1600's, kings and other noblemen often hired musicians to work in their courts. One popular type of courtly music was the lute song. These songs, usually about love, were accompanied by the *lute*, an instrument similar to the guitar. The text of *Love in Thy Youth* was probably used for a lute song in a nobleman's court.

As you prepare to perform *Love In Thy Youth*:
• Look through the song and become familiar with the key of F major.
• Notice the places where the melody outlines the intervals of the tonic chord.
• Find the section of the song that is monophonic (unison melody). Find the section that is homophonic (parts that share the same or nearly the same rhythm, but on different pitches). Find the section that is polyphonic (parts have different rhythms).
• Read the rhythm, then add the pitch, and repeat as needed.
• Add the text and sing musically using good vowels, diphthongs, and articulation.

AS THE HOLLY GROWETH GREEN
Tenor Bass Chorus

History: Like the song for treble chorus described above, this song for tenor bass chorus *As the Holly Groweth Green* was probably a *lute* song. Sometimes kings would write their own texts or songs for their musicians to perform. King Henry VIII of England wrote the text of *As the Holly Groweth Green*.

As you prepare to sing *As The Holly Groweth Green*:
• Look through the song to become familiar with the key of F major.
• Find the places where the melody outlines the intervals of the tonic chord.
• Notice the call-response between the tenor and bass, in measure 43 on "adieu" (pronounced ah-d(ee)oo, the French word for "good-bye").
• Read the rhythm, add the pitch, repeat as needed.
• Add the text and sing musically, using good vowels, diphthongs, and articulation.

TREBLE CHORUS

Love In Thy Youth

For SA a cappella

Anonymous, 17th Century

Music by
EMILY CROCKER

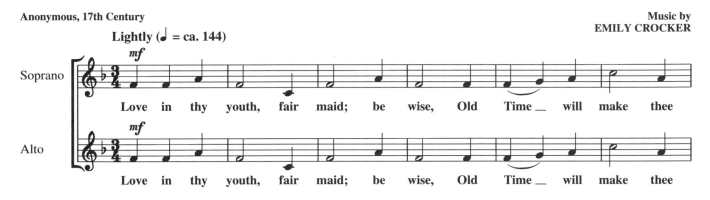

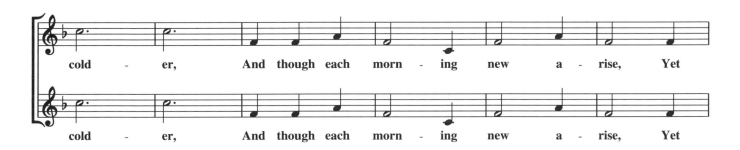

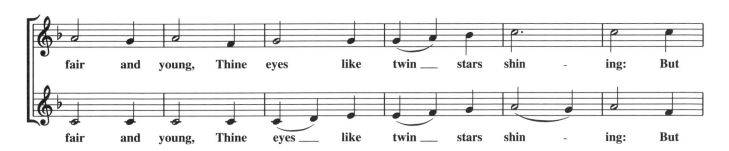

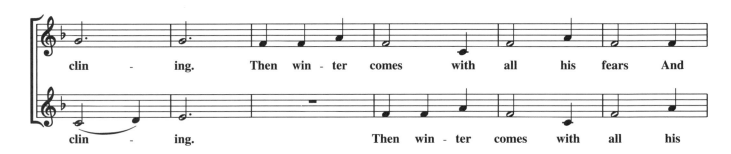

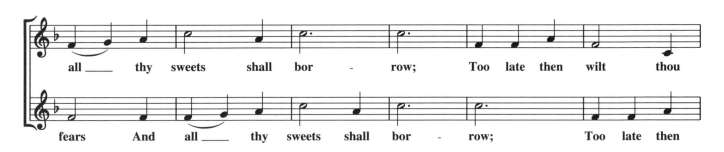

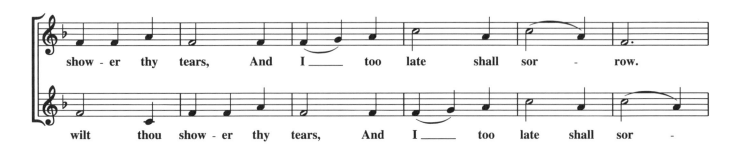

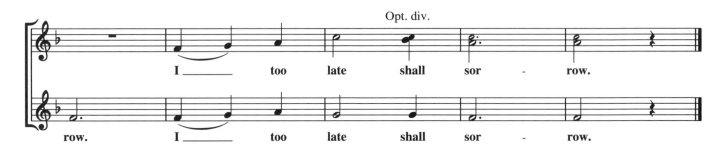

TENOR BASS CHORUS

As the Holly Groweth Green

For TB a cappella

KING HENRY VIII

Music by
EMILY CROCKER

la - dy Prom - ise to her ___ I make, From all

la - dy ___ Prom - ise to her I make, From all

oth - er on - ly to her I me ___ be - take.

oth - er on - ly to her I me be - take.

A - dieu, a - dieu, a - dieu my

A - dieu, a - dieu, a - dieu my

la - dy, a - dieu. Who hath my heart ___ tru -

la - dy, a - dieu. Who hath my heart ___ tru -

ly, be sure, and ev - er shall.

ly, be sure, and ev - er shall.

MIXED CHORUS

Musical Terms:

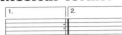

First and second endings. A repeated section; the first time, sing the first ending; the second time, skip the first ending and go to the second ending.

As you prepare to perform *The Call*:
- Find the places where there is an interval skip in the F major tonic chord.
- Notice the quarter rest on the first beat of each phrase.
- Add the text and sing musically, using good vowels, diphthongs, and articulation.

The Call

For SATB a cappella

Words by GEORGE HERBERT (1593-1633)

Music by JOHN LEAVITT

POSTURE/BREATH

1. Stand in your best singing posture. Imagine there is a balloon attached to the top of your head. Allow the balloon to bring your head into alignment with your spine.

2. Exhale your air on an "ss" like air escaping from a tire. On a signal from your director, stop the air, and notice the breath support from the diaphragm.

3. Imagine that as you inhale you are filling a balloon with air. Inhale over 8 counts, exhale on a "ss."

ARTICULATION

In our daily speech we are often careless about pronouncing all the sounds of all the words:

I gotta go home now. Are ya goin' t' the dance? Who ya goin' with?

In choral singing, however, it's important to articulate the diction clearly. Otherwise the performance will sound ragged and sloppy. Here are a few exercises to practice articulation. Speak each phrase first, then sing it on a repeated unison pitch or scale pattern.

"t" and "d"
Both consonants are produced with the tip of the tongue, but "t" is "unvoiced" and "d" is "voiced." Notice that sometimes the "t" sound is used even when there is no "t" in the word: *laughed* is pronounced *laft.*

4. Repeat the following "t" patterns:
   - *t t t t t t t t*
   - *Tiptoe through the tulips*
   - *Two times ten is twenty*
   - *He laughed. She talked. We worked. They hoped.*

5. Repeat the following:
   - *d d d d d d d*
   - *day by day*
   - *dream a dream*
   - *do or die*

ARTICULATION

"t" and "d" before a vowel

When "t" or "d" is followed by a syllable or word beginning with a vowel, connect the "t" with that vowel:

- *What a surprise!*
- *Wait until tomorrow.*
- *Sweet is the sound.*
- *The winding road*
- *Open the window*
- *Ride off into the sunset*

"t" and "d" before a consonant

Even though in speaking, we often drop a "t" or "d" before a consonant, singing it that way would sound careless. Practice these consonant sounds, followed by the same sound on a short phrase:

- *t-b, t-b, t-b*   *might belong, might belong*
- *t-d, t-d, t-d*   *sweet dessert, sweet dessert*
- *t-f, t-f, t-f*   *Is it free? Is it free?*
- *d-m, d-m, d-m*   *We could meet you there.*
- *d-th, d-th, d-th*   *Sound the trumpet*

"t" followed by another "t" — "d" followed by another "d"

Most of the time when a "t" or "d" is followed by another "t" or "d", you will want to pronounce only one of them.

- *I went to see the doctor.*
- *Come at ten o'clock.*
- *We had a great time.*
- *Pretty as a picture*
- *Written on the wall*
- *Hey diddle diddle, the cat and the fiddle*

"t" followed by an "s"

Most of the time, you will want to connect the "t" with the "s".

- *sweet song*
- *great sound*
- *street sign*
- *Mozart sonata*
- *short story*

EIGHTH NOTES AND RESTS

So far, we've used whole, half, and quarter notes. An *eighth note* (♪) is half the value of a quarter note. Two eighth notes (♫) have the same duration as one quarter note. The eighth note has a corresponding rest, the eighth rest (⁊) which shares the same length as an eighth note.

Below is a chart summarizing the notes and rests we've learned.

	note	rest
whole	o	▬
half	♩	▬
quarter	♩	𝄽
eighth	♪	⁊

The following diagram summarizes the relationships between the notes we've studied:

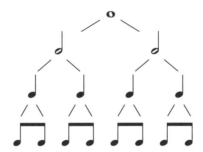

More about eighth notes

If the quarter note receives the beat, you can consider eighth notes to be a division of the beat:

Eighth notes may be notated singly with a stem and a flag:

Or they may be beamed together in groups:

Check your knowledge!

1. How many *eighth notes* equal a quarter note? A half note? A whole note?

2. Describe two ways eighth notes can be notated.

RHYTHM PRACTICE

Read each line (clap, tap, or chant).

EIGHTH NOTE PRACTICE

Clap, tap, or chant each line.

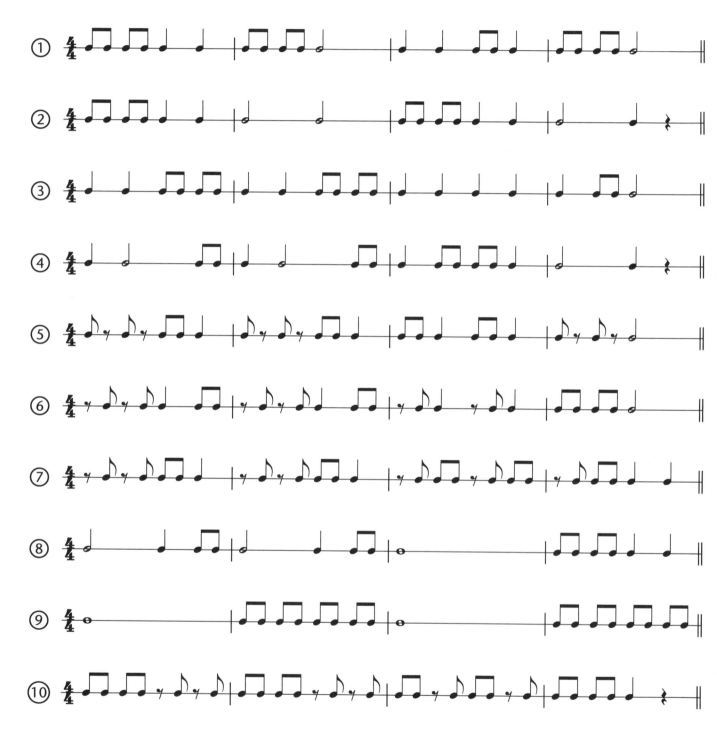

SPEECH CHORUS

History: *Hey Diddle Diddle!* is an English nursery rhyme. Sometimes these rhymes are called "Mother Goose" rhymes, but no one knows exactly why. We don't know who made them up or when they began. Rhymes for little children like this one exist in many different languages and cultures around the world.

As you prepare to perform *Hey Diddle Diddle!*
• Read the rhythm of each part.
• Combine the parts.
• Add the text. Repeat to increase the tempo.
• Add the dynamics, and concentrate on the articulation and diction, especially the "t" and "d" sounds.

Hey Diddle Diddle!

For 2-Part Speech Chorus

English Nursery Rhyme

Music by
EMILY CROCKER

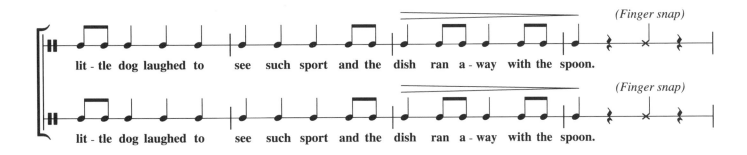

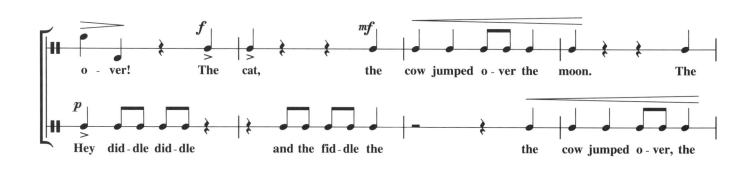

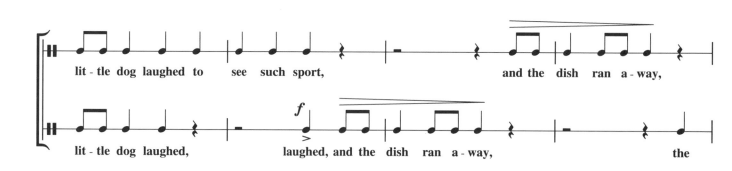

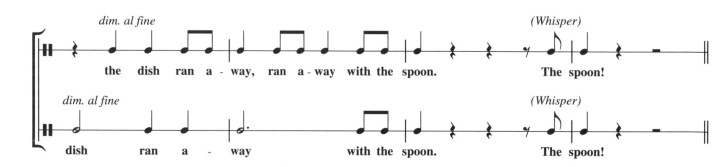

REVIEW AND PRACTICE

1. What is a *diphthong*?

2. Describe how to sing the vowel sounds in the following diphthongs:
   I   my   day   joy   now   way   though

3. How do you perform the "t" or "d" in the following phrases?
   - *Wait until dark*
   - *The winding road*

4. In the following phrases, how do you sound the "t" or "d" when singing?
   - *Great day!*
   - *Sound the trumpet*

5. In the following phrases with double "t" or "d" sounds, do you sound both of them when singing?
   - *Hey diddle diddle*
   - *Come at ten o'clock*

6. How do you perform a "t" or "d" followed by an "s"?
   - *Sweet sounds*
   - *Ends so soon*

Apply your knowledge by singing the following exercises:

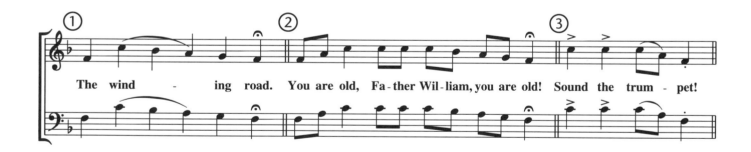

REVIEW AND PRACTICE

Check your knowledge!

1. How many beat(s) does an eighth note receive in a meter of $\frac{4}{4}$?

2. How many eighth notes take up a whole measure of $\frac{3}{4}$ meter? $\frac{2}{4}$ meter? $\frac{4}{4}$ meter?

3. How many quarter notes take up a whole measure of $\frac{3}{4}$ meter? $\frac{2}{4}$ meter? $\frac{4}{4}$ meter?

4. How many half notes take up a whole measure of $\frac{3}{4}$ meter? $\frac{2}{4}$ meter? $\frac{4}{4}$ meter?

5. What number of eighth notes equals the duration of a half note? A whole note?

6. What one note value completely fills a measure of $\frac{4}{4}$ meter? Of $\frac{3}{4}$? Of $\frac{2}{4}$?

7. What note value receives the beat in $\frac{4}{4}$ meter?

8. How many beats does a whole rest receive in $\frac{4}{4}$ meter? A half rest? A quarter rest? An eighth rest?

9. Assuming a meter of $\frac{3}{4}$, how many eighth notes are in the song *Happy Birthday to You*?

10. Supply a meter for the following rhythm patterns:

PRACTICE WITH EIGHTH NOTES

Read each line separately and in any combination. Describe the time and key signature.

TREBLE CHORUS

History: In the late 19th and early 20th century, interest began to grow in folk music. Cecil Sharpe in the British Isles, John Jacob Niles and John Lomax in the United States, Bela Bartok and Zoltan Kodály in Hungary, and others traveled back roads and country lanes writing down tunes sung by the people they met along the way.

As the work of these musical pioneers became known, composers began to use folk music as source material for symphonies, ballet scores, operas, songs and chamber music. In America, Aaron Copland and Virgil Thomson were two well-known composers who made use of American folk music. In Hungary, Kodály, in addition to his work in cataloging folk music and composing, became known as a leader in music education. *Let Us Chase The Squirrel* is an example of a simple American folksong arranged using Kodály techniques.

As you prepare to perform *Let Us Chase The Squirrel*:
• Discover which sections are monophonic, which are homophonic, and which are polyphonic.
• Identify the key, and notice the places where there are interval skips. Take special care to distinguish the descending intervals from the tonic: F to E, and F to C.
• Read the rhythm of each part, then add the pitch. When the parts are secure, combine them into two (or optionally three) parts.
• Add dynamics and perform expressively.

Let Us Chase The Squirrel

For SA or SSA a cappella

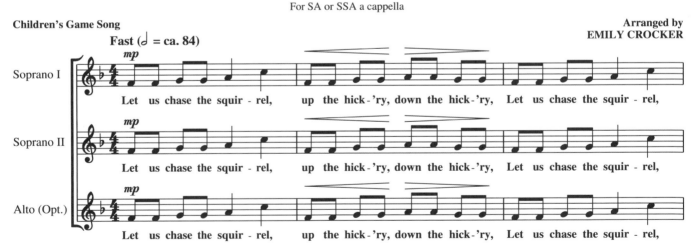

TENOR BASS CHORUS

History: Sea Chanteys were songs sung by sailors in rhythm with their work. Work on board a ship was very hard, and different kinds of songs developed for pulling ropes and other tasks.

Leave Her, Johnny is a variation of two earlier sea chanteys: *Leave Her, Bullies, Leave Her* and *Across the Western Ocean*. The song dates to about 1850 when thousands left Ireland after the potato famine forced them to flee the economic hardship of their native land.

As you prepare to perform *Leave Her, Johnny*:
- Identify the key and time signatures, and notice where the melody has interval skips.
- Read the rhythm, then add pitch, and repeat until the parts are secure.
- Sing in two (or optionally three) parts, and add the text. Sing with expression.

Leave Her, Johnny

For TB or TTB a cappella

Traditional Sea Chantey

Arranged by
EMILY CROCKER

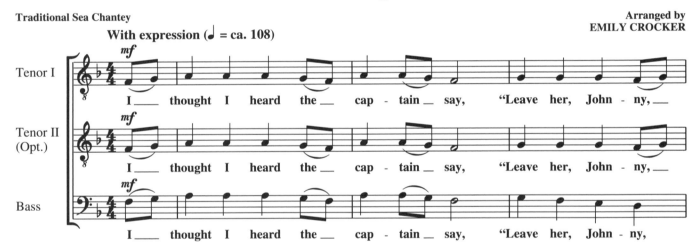

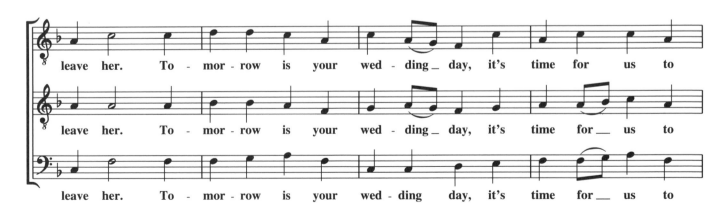

leave _ her." The _ trip was hard and the wind was _ strong, Leave her, John - ny, _

leave _ her." The _ trip was hard and the wind was _ strong, Leave her, John - ny, _

leave her." The _ trip was hard and the wind was _ strong, Leave her, John - ny,

leave her. But you'll be back be - fore e'er _ long, It's time for us to

leave her. But you'll be back be - fore e'er _ long, It's time for _ us to

leave her. But you'll be back be - fore e'er long, It's time for _ us to

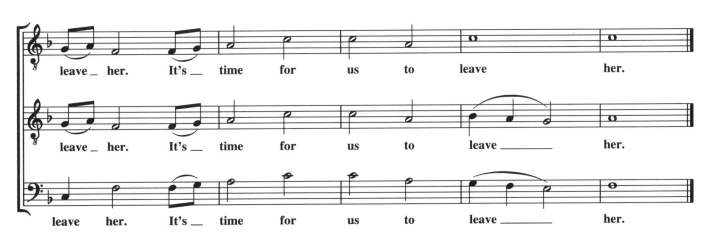

leave _ her. It's _ time for us to leave her.

leave _ her. It's _ time for us to leave _____ her.

leave her. It's _ time for us to leave _____ her.

 MIXED CHORUS

This traditional rhyme has been set to music in such a way that the humor of the text is emphasized. As you prepare to perform Betty Botter:
- Notice the places where the melody outlines the intervals of the tonic chord.
- Notice the 2- measure rest in both the SA and TB. Be sure to count and listen to the other parts so you come in on the right pitch at the right time.
- Chant the text in rhythm, concentrating on articulation. Use expression!

Betty Botter

For SATB a cappella

Traditional Rhyme

Music by
JOHN LEAVITT

POSTURE/BREATH

Posture: Check your posture and ask yourself these questions.
- Stand with feet apart (Is your weight balanced?)
- Knees unlocked (Can you bend them easily?)
- Back straight (Are you standing erect comfortably and not stiff?)
- Head erect (Is your chin level, and not too far up or down?)
- Rib cage lifted (Is your chest high and able to expand?)
- Shoulders relaxed (Are they comfortably down, not too far forward or back?)
- Hands at your side (Are they relaxed and free of tension?)

Remember that just like athletes, singers need to prepare themselves for the physical process of singing. Performance, whether on the playing field or in a concert will suffer if the body is not sufficiently prepared or involved.

Practice good posture, good breathing, and good vocal habits every day in rehearsal, and these good habits will be there to help you succeed in performance.

1. Lift the left shoulder high and let it fall. Repeat with the right shoulder and finally both shoulders. Stretch overhead, fall forward like a rag doll, and gradually stand up to a good singing posture.

Breath: Practice breathing exercises every day. Apply this practice to all your music making, sight-reading music, rehearsing music, performing music.

2. When people are suddenly startled, they usually take a deep natural breath very quickly. Take a "surprised" breath. Notice the action of the *diaphragm*.

3. Imagine that there is an elevator platform at the bottom of your lungs. Drop the platform toward the floor as you inhale. Inhale 4 counts, exhale 4 counts. Repeat with 5, then 6 counts.

ARTICULATION
Singing the consonant "r"
There are two kinds of "r" sounds which are used in singing in English. The American "r" is the "r" which is used in daily speech. The flipped "r" could be described by the saying "very good" sounding as "veddy good" as they say it in England (the tip of the tongue at the back of the front teeth). Both are used in singing.

In singing, we must carefully prepare the articulation of words containing "r" sounds. This is because an "r" can affect the vowel sound which it precedes or follows. Say or sing the word "care" on a unison pitch, holding the vowel and gradually changing to the "r" sound: "kehrrrrrr _____". Did you notice the movement of the tongue and the change in the sound?

ARTICULATION

Guidelines for singing "r"

Whether you choose to sing an American "r" or a flipped "r" will depend on the kind of music you are singing. It is important, however, for an ensemble to have a uniform sound on an "r", since even 1 or 2 voices can affect the sound of the entire group.

Sing "r" before a vowel: This holds true whether the "r" is in the same word with the vowel, or in adjoining words. Practice the following examples and repeat at different pitch levels.

De-emphasize "r" before a consonant: This can be a challenging concept for anyone learning to sing, but a necessary one in developing a pleasing choral tone quality. There are some exceptions to this practice, mostly in popular music and certain kinds of solo work, but in general, the rule applies. Practice the following examples, omitting the "r" sound when it precedes a consonant.

MORE ABOUT METER

Remember that *meter* is a form of rhythmic organization. In the simple meters we have been using, the top number indicates the number of beats per measure in the music. The bottom number indicates which note value receives the beat.

4 = Four beats per measure (♩ ♩ ♩ ♩)
4 = The quarter note (♩) receives the beat

3 = Three beats per measure (♩ ♩ ♩)
4 = The quarter note (♩) receives the beat

2 = Two beats per measure (♩ ♩)
4 = The quarter note (♩) receives the beat

So that the ear can easily recognize and group notes into the various meters, each meter stresses certain beats. Almost all meters stress the first beat of each measure. This is called the downbeat.

In $\frac{4}{4}$ meter, a secondary stress occurs on beat three along with the stressed downbeat.

Check your knowledge!
1. Define *meter*.

2. Describe the following meters: $\frac{3}{4}$, $\frac{2}{4}$, $\frac{4}{4}$.

3. What is a *downbeat*?

4. What beats are stressed in $\frac{4}{4}$ meter? In $\frac{3}{4}$ meter? In $\frac{2}{4}$ meter?

CHANGING METERS

Read the following exercise with changing meters. Clap, tap, or chant.

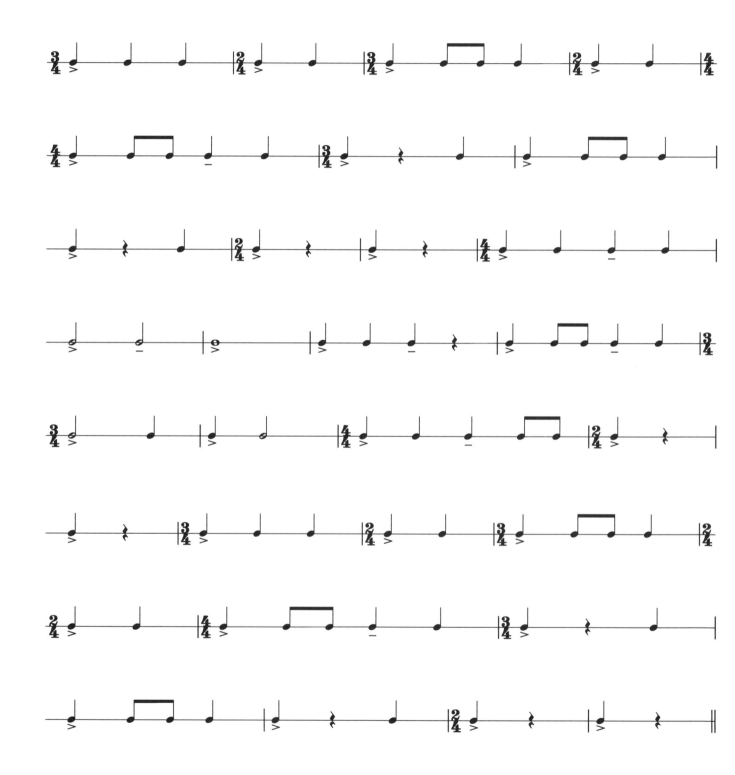

TREBLE • TENOR BASS • MIXED

History: Music with changing meters has been widely used throughout history and in various cultures. During the Renaissance, meters shifted easily from meter groupings of 2 beats to groupings of 3. During the period from 1600-1900 metrical patterns became more regular, although Bach, Beethoven, Brahms, and others used techniques which interrupted the regular pulse. Brahms wrote a famous work *Variations*, Op. 21, No.2 which was written in $\frac{3}{4} + \frac{4}{4}$.

By the 20th century, composers became interested in more variety in rhythm and meter as a compositional technique. Works for all kinds of ensembles were written with changing meters and other interesting rhythmic effects. There are many famous works which use changing meters including Igor Stravinsky's *Danse sacral* from *The Rite of Spring* and Carl Orff's *Carmina Burana*.

Music from other cultures including music of the Middle East, Eastern Europe and Indian ragas are often organized with complex meters and other rhythmic devices.

As you prepare to perform *Alleluia*:
- Identify the time signatures throughout the piece. Identify the key.
- Read through the rhythm. Stress the downbeats and other secondary beats in each measure as they occur.
- Notice the places where the melody outlines the intervals of tonic chord. Can you identify the tonic chord when it occurs?
- Add the pitch, and repeat as needed for accuracy.
- Add the text, and work to increase the tempo. (De-emphasize the "r" in the word "together," i.e. sing as *too-GEH-thuh*)
- Sing with energy and expression.

Alleluia

For SA, TB, or SATB a cappella

Music by
JOHN LEAVITT

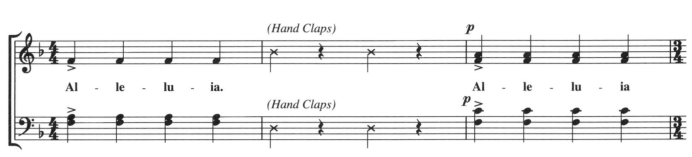

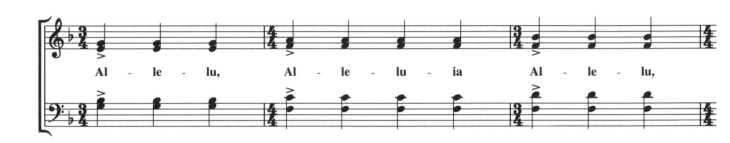

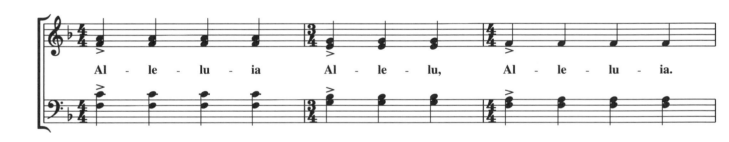

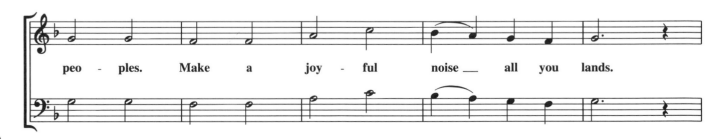

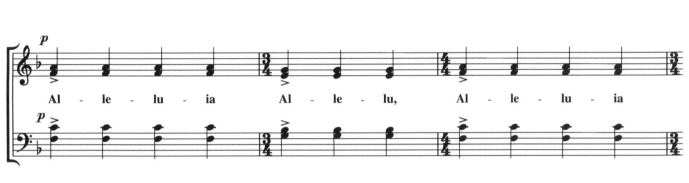

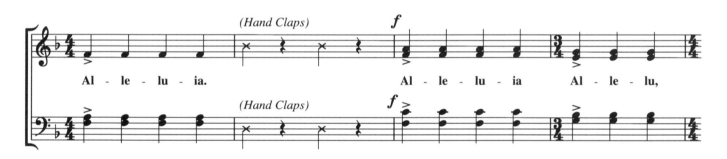

COMPREHENSIVE REVIEW

Answer the following questions orally in large or small group discussion.

1. Why is good posture important in singing?

2. Describe the steps for a good singing posture.

3. Describe a good singing posture for singing from memory. Describe a good singing posture for holding music. For sharing music with another singer.

4. Why do we need *articulation* in singing? What are the *articulators*?

5. What are the three stages of breathing for singing?

6. Describe the action of the *diaphragm* during breathing. The abdomen. The ribs. The lungs.

7. How does an expanded rib cage affect breath capacity?

8. What are the five basic vowel sounds? Describe the basic formation of each.

9. What is the general rule for producing other vowel sounds in addition to the five basic vowel sounds?

10. What is the *neutral* vowel?

11. Describe the difference in the vowel sounds of the following:
    - 2nd syllable of *welcome*
    - 1st syllable of *Alleluia*

12. What is the source of *vocal tone*? What is it popularly called?

13. How do the vocal folds produce sound?

14. What is a *diphthong*? Describe and demonstrate how to sing the following diphthongs: *light   bright   you   I   why   now*

15. Describe and demonstrate the pronunciation of the following words using the consonants "t", "d", and "r":
    Dream a dream   Sweet music   Rejoice!   Dark brown is the river

COMPREHENSIVE REVIEW

Check your knowledge!

1.   What is *rhythm*?

2.   Define *beat*.

3.   How many half notes equal the same duration as a whole note?

4.   How many quarter notes equal the same duration as a half note?

5.   How many quarter notes equal the same duration as a whole note?

6.   How many lines and spaces make up a *staff*?

7.   Give both names for the *clefs* we've learned and describe them.

8.   Name the pitch which may be written on its own little line in either clef.

9.   When treble clef notes are written in the bass clef or bass clef notes are written in the treble clef, they use additional little lines as in #8. What are these lines called?

10. What are the vertical lines that divide a staff into smaller sections called?

11. Name the smaller divided sections of a staff.

12. How can you tell the end of a section or piece of music?

13. Describe *meter*.

14. What are the numbers that identify the meter called?

15. Describe the following meters: $\frac{4}{4}$, $\frac{3}{4}$, $\frac{2}{4}$

16. What is another name for musical notes?

17. Define *scale*. What is the Italian word for scale and its definition?

18. Describe *key*. Describe *keynote*.

19. What is the difference between a *whole step* and a *half step*?

COMPREHENSIVE REVIEW

20. What is a *major scale*?

21. What is the order of whole/half steps in a major scale?

22. What is a *slur*?

23. Where does the word *pianoforte* come from and what does it mean?

24. Describe *f* *p* *mf* *mp*. What are these signs called?

25. What is an octave?

26. Define *soprano, alto, tenor, bass*.

27. What is an *interval*? What is the difference between *melodic* and *harmonic* intervals?

28. What is a *chord*?

29. How many tones are needed to form a chord?

30. What is the difference between a *chord* and a *triad*?

31. What is another name for *keynote*?

32. On what tone of the major scale is a tonic chord built?

33. Describe the key signature for C major, G major, and F major.

34. How many beat(s) does an eighth note receive in a meter of $\frac{4}{4}$?

35. What number of eighth notes equals the duration of a half note? A whole note?

36. What is a *downbeat*?

37. What beats are stressed in $\frac{4}{4}$ meter? In $\frac{3}{4}$ meter? In $\frac{2}{4}$ meter?

38. What is the dotted note rule?

TREBLE CHORUS

Oh, Soldier, Soldier

For SA and Piano

Traditional Text

Music by
EMILY CROCKER

TREBLE CHORUS

no, sweet maid, I can-not mar-ry thee, for I have no coat to put on." Then up she went to her
(hat)
(boots)

no, sweet maid, I can-not mar-ry thee, for I have no coat to put on." Then up she went to her
(hat)
(boots)

grand-fa-ther's chest, and got him a coat of the ver-y best. "Oh
(hat)
(some boots)

grand-fa-ther's chest, and got him a coat of the ver-y best. "Oh
(hat)
(some boots)

TREBLE CHORUS

3rd time molto rit.

sol - dier, sol - dier, won't you mar - ry me, for you have a coat of your own."
(hat)
(some boots)

3rd time molto rit.

sol - dier, sol - dier, won't you mar - ry me, for you have a coat of your own."
(hat)
(some boots)

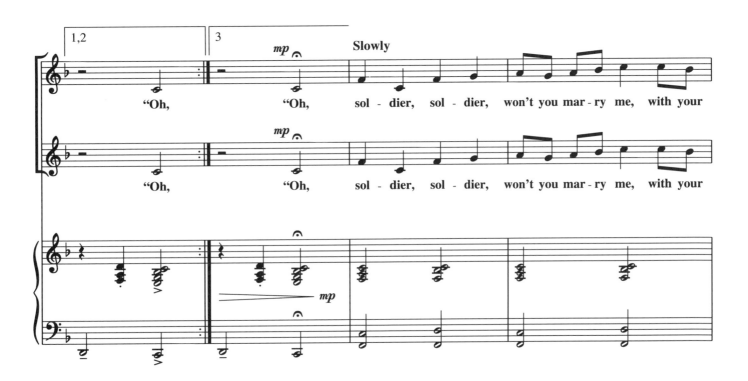

"Oh, "Oh, sol - dier, sol - dier, won't you mar - ry me, with your

"Oh, "Oh, sol - dier, sol - dier, won't you mar - ry me, with your

TREBLE CHORUS

Tempo I

rit. f

mus - ket, fife, and drum?" "Oh no, sweet maid, I can - not mar - ry thee, for I

mus - ket, fife, and drum?" "Oh no, sweet maid, I can - not mar - ry thee, for I

div.

have a wife at home."

have a wife at ____ home."

TENOR BASS CHORUS

The Hunt

For TB and Piano

Traditional American (adapted)

Music by
EMILY CROCKER

With horns and hounds in _ cho-rus, let's ush-er in the day. With horns and hounds in _

TENOR BASS CHORUS

cho - rus, let's ush - er in the day. The sport's ex - ceed - ing

glo - ri - ous, a - rise, make no de - lay. The sun shines now up -

a - rise, make no de - lay, de - lay.

161

The Bells

For SATB and Piano

Words by
EDGAR ALLEN POE

Music by
JOHN LEAVITT

MIXED CHORUS

MIXED CHORUS

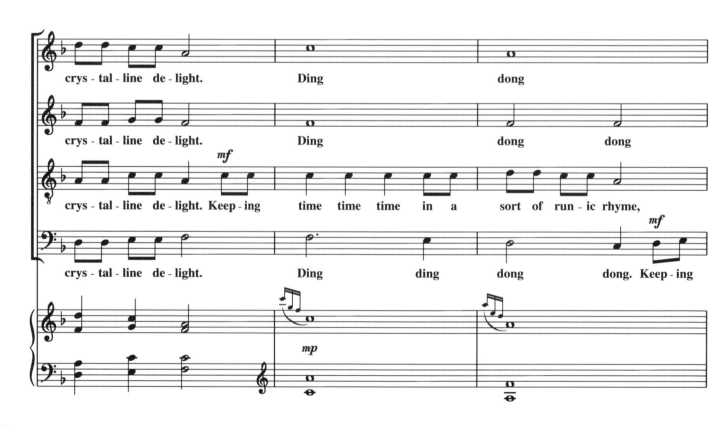

MIXED CHORUS

SOLFEGE

(Movable "do")
"Do" changes as the key changes.

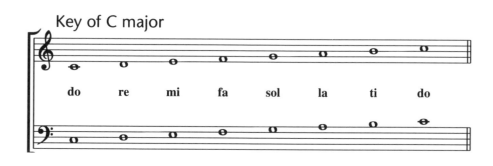

Key of C major

do   re   mi   fa   sol   la   ti   do

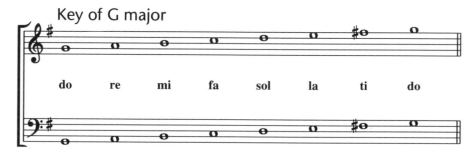

Key of G major

do   re   mi   fa   sol   la   ti   do

Movable "do" — Accidentals (in all keys)

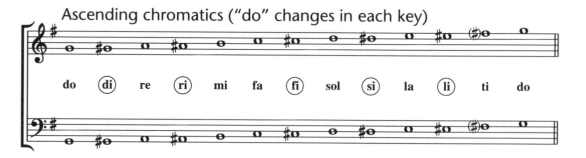

Ascending chromatics ("do" changes in each key)

do (di) re (ri) mi fa (fi) sol (si) la (li) ti do

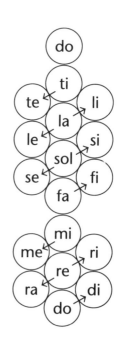

Descending chromatics ("do" changes in each key)

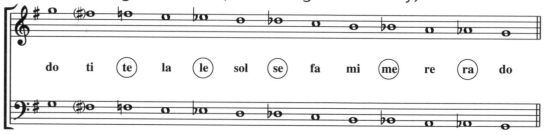

do ti (te) la (le) sol (se) fa mi (me) re (ra) do

 SOLFEGE

(Fixed "do")
"Do" is C and the pitch syllables remain fixed no matter what the key.

Key of C major

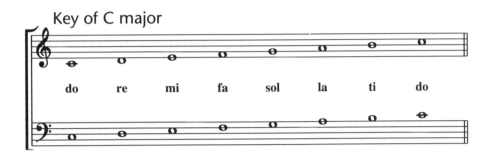

Key of F major

Fixed "do"
Accidentals are fixed as follows:

Ascending chromatics

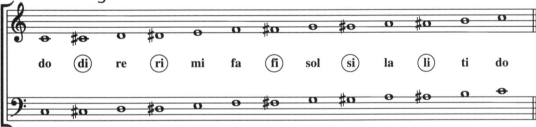

Descending chromatics

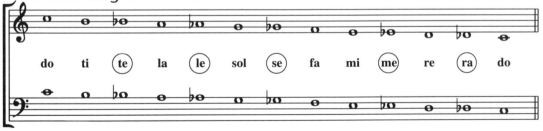

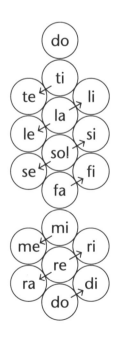

NUMBERS

Numbers (pitch)
Like movable "do," the "1" changes with each key.

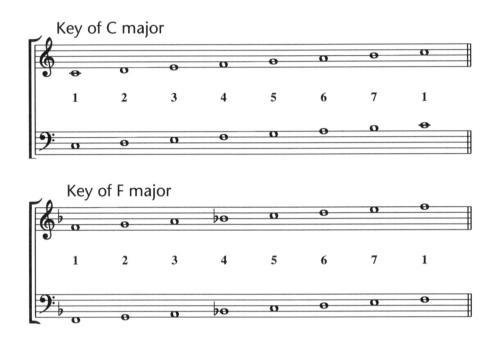

Accidentals can be performed either by singing the number but raising or lowering the pitch by a half step, or by singing the word "sharp" or "flat" before the number as a grace note.

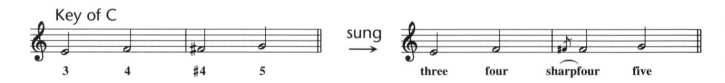

COUNTING SYSTEMS - SIMPLE METER

There are several systems in use which are quite effective. Here are three:

Kodály	Traditional	Eastman

Row 1: 4/4

Kodály: ta ta ta ta

Traditional: 1 2 3 4

Eastman: 1 2 3 4

Row 2: 4/4

Kodály: ta _____ ta _____

Traditional: 1 _____ 3 _____

Eastman: 1 _____ 3 _____

Row 3: 4/4

Kodály: ta _____

Traditional: 1 _____

Eastman: 1 _____

Row 4: 4/4

Kodály: ti ti ti ti ti ti ti ti

Traditional: 1 & 2 & 3 & 4 &

Eastman: 1 te 2 te 3 te 4 te

Row 5: 4/4

Kodály: ti ri ti ri ti ri ti ri ti ri ti ri ti ri ti ri

Traditional: 1 e & a 2 e & a 3 e & a 4 e & a

Eastman: 1 ta te ta 2 ta te ta 3 ta te ta 4 ta te ta

Row 6: 4/4

Kodály: ti ti ri ti ti ri ti ti ri ti ti ri

Traditional: 1 & a 2 & a 3 & a 4 & a

Eastman: 1 te ta 2 te ta 3 te ta 4 te ta

COUNTING SYSTEMS

Kodály	Traditional	Eastman
(Beat) 4/4 ti ri ti · ti ri ti · ti ri ti · ti ri ti	4/4 1 e & · 2 e & · 3 e & · 4 e &	4/4 1 ta te · 2 ta te · 3 ta te · 4 ta te
(Beat) 4/4 ta _____ ta	4/4 1 _____ 4	4/4 1 _____ 4
(Beat) 4/4 ta · i ti ta · i ti	4/4 1 _____ & 3 _____ &	4/4 1 _____ te 3 _____ te
(Beat) 4/4 tim ri tim ri tim ri tim ri	4/4 1 a 2 a 3 a 4 a	4/4 1 ta 2 ta 3 ta 4 ta
(Beat) 4/4 tir im tir im tir im tir im	4/4 1 e 2 e 3 e 4 e	4/4 1 ta 2 ta 3 ta 4 ta
(Beat) 4/4 ta ta ta ta _____ ta _____	4/4 1 2 3 4 _____ 3 _____	4/4 1 2 3 4 _____ 3 _____
(Beat) 4/4 ta ta _____ ta	4/4 1 2 _____ 4	4/4 1 2 _____ 4
(Beat) 4/4 syn - co - pa syn - co - pa (or ti ta ti)	4/4 1 & _____ & 3 & _____ &	4/4 1 te _____ te 3 te _____ te
(Beat) 4/4 tir im ri tir im ri tir im ri tir im ri	4/4 1 e a 2 e a 3 e a 4 e a	4/4 1 ta ta 2 ta ta 3 ta ta 4 ta ta

OTHER SIMPLE METERS

Adapt the information from the charts on pages 169-170 to apply to music in other simple meters:

Simple Meters: Simple meters are based upon the note which receives the beat, i.e. $\frac{4}{4}$ meter is based upon the quarter note receiving the beat.

2 = 2 beats per measure (♪ ♪)
8 = The eighth note (♪) receives the beat

3 = 3 beats per measure (♪ ♪ ♪)
8 = The eighth note (♪) receives the beat

4 = 4 beats per measure (♪ ♪ ♪ ♪)
8 = The eighth note (♪) receives the beat

2 = 2 beats per measure (♩ ♩)
2 = The half note (♩) receives the beat   (Note: sometimes written as ¢ "cut time")

3 = 3 beats per measure (♩ ♩ ♩)
2 = The half note (♩) receives the beat

4 = 4 beats per measure (♩ ♩ ♩ ♩)
2 = The half note (♩) receives the beat.

 COMPOUND METER

Kodály	Traditional	Eastman
(Beat) — — / ti ti ti ti ti ti / (or tri - ple - ti tri - ple - ti)	$\frac{6}{8}$ — — / 1 2 3 4 5 6	$\frac{6}{8}$ — — / 1 la li 2 la li
(Beat) / $\frac{6}{8}$ ta ti ta ti	$\frac{6}{8}$ 1 3 4 6	$\frac{6}{8}$ 1 li 2 li
(Beat) / $\frac{6}{8}$ ta____i ta____i	$\frac{6}{8}$ 1_____ 4_____	$\frac{6}{8}$ 1_____ 2_____
(Beat) / $\frac{6}{8}$ ta_____	$\frac{6}{8}$ 1_____	$\frac{6}{8}$ 1_____

OTHER COMPOUND METERS

Adapt the information from the above charts to apply to music in other compound meters.

Compound Meters: Compound meters are meters which have a multiple of 3, such as 6 or 9 (but not 3 itself). Unlike simple meter which reflects the note that receives the beat, compound meter reflects the note that receives the division.

To determine the note that receives the beat, add three divisions together. For example:

6 = 6 divisions to the measure (2 groups of 3)
8 = The eighth note receives the division
        (the dotted quarter receives the beat)

9 = 9 divisions to the measure (3 groups of 3)
8 = The eighth note receives the division
        (the dotted quarter receives the beat)

12 = 12 divisions to the measure (4 groups of 3)
4 = The quarter note receives the division
        (the dotted half note receives the beat)

An exception to this compound meter rule is when the music occurs at a slow tempo, then the music is felt in beats, rather than divisions.

RHYTHM DRILLS

Simple Meter

The rhythmic, melodic, and harmonic exercises on the following pages are included for reference or drill as needed.

Beat, Division, and Subdivision

Clap, tap, or chant each line

 RHYTHM DRILLS

Dotted Rhythms
Clap, tap, or chant each line

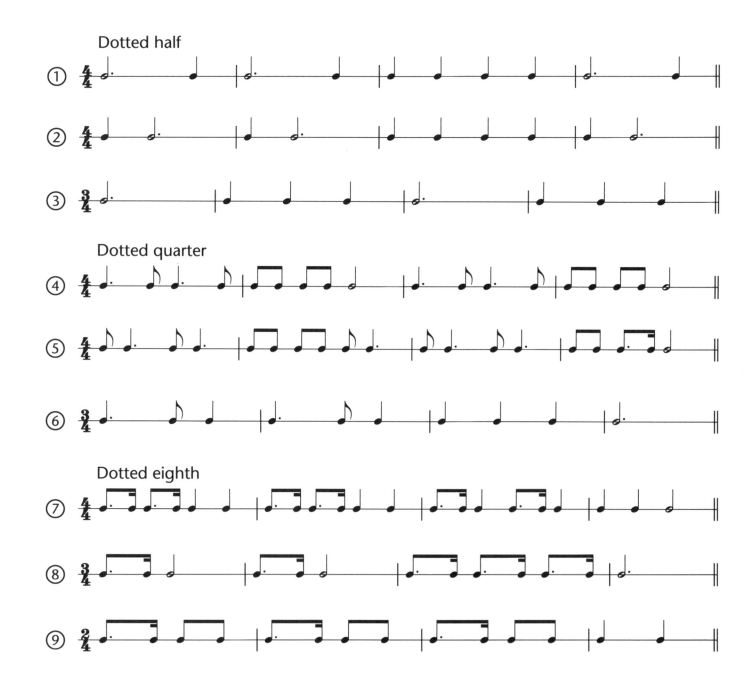

RHYTHM DRILLS

Compound Meter

Clap, tap, or chant each line.
What note gets the beat? The division?

Dotted patterns

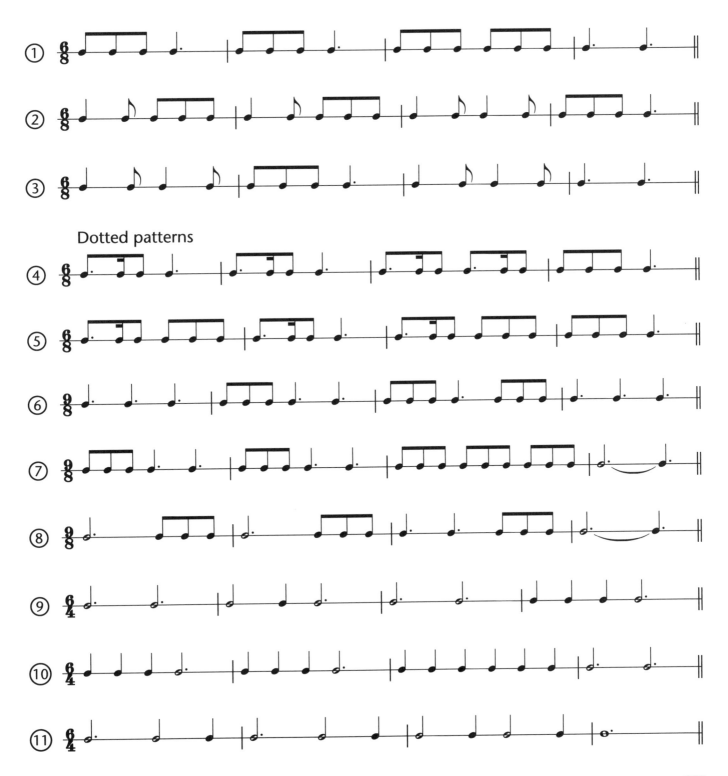

PITCH DRILLS

Key of D Major

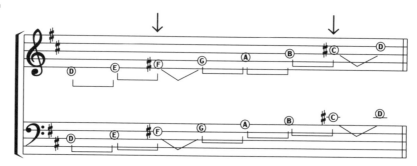

Chord–builders

Chord Drills

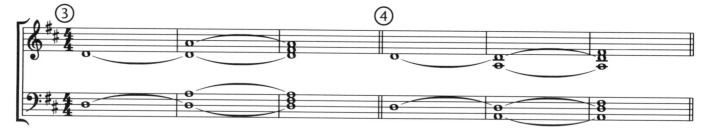

Sing separately and in any combination.

PITCH DRILLS

Key of B Flat Major

Chord–builders

Chord Drills

Sing separately and in any combination.

ABOUT THE AUTHORS

EMILY HOLT CROCKER is a native Texan and was a professional educator for 15 years. She taught all levels of choral music, specializing in middle school/junior high, where her choirs received numerous superior ratings in concert and sight-reading competitions. In 1989, she joined the music publishing industry and in 1992 was named Director of Choral Publications for Hal Leonard Corporation in Milwaukee, Wisconsin. She holds degrees from the University of North Texas and Texas Woman's University and has done additional post-graduate work at the University of North Texas, where she was assistant conductor of the A Cappella Choir and taught music education.

She is the founder and director of the Milwaukee Children's Choir, a group that was organized in 1994 and is sponsored by the Milwaukee Chamber Orchestra.

Ms. Crocker is known nationally as one of the premier choral writers specializing in music for young choirs. She has over one hundred works currently in print and since 1986 has been awarded ASCAP special awards for Educational and Concert music. In addition to her responsibilities at Hal Leonard, she maintains a busy guest conducting, workshop, and writing schedule each year.

JOHN LEAVITT is a Kansas native, born and raised in Leavenworth, Kansas. He completed doctoral work in Choral Conducting at the University of Missouri-Kansas City Conservatory of Music.

His undergraduate work is in music education from Emporia State University. After graduation, Dr. Leavitt moved to Wichita, Kansas where he worked in television for five years. At Wichita State University, he pursued a Master of Music degree in piano performance with significant study in composition.

While in Wichita, he directed the parish music program at Immanuel Lutheran Church and served on the faculty at Friends University where he won the faculty award for teaching excellence in 1989. In the fall of 1992, Dr. Leavitt accepted a one year teaching appointment with Concordia College in Edmonton, Alberta, Canada, where he was director of choral activities and assistant professor of music.

Returning in 1993 to Wichita, he now devotes himself to full-time composing and conducting. He is the artistic director and conductor of a professionally trained vocal ensemble known as The Master Arts Chorale and an associated Children's Choir, The Master Arts Youth Chorale.

Dr. Leavitt's works receive wide acclaim and he has received ASCAP awards since 1991. In addition to his busy guest conducting and workshop schedule, he writes many commissioned works each year.